To be successful at senior lev___, _____ *tively work with peers who may have competing priorities. Unite! provides a roadmap to navigate this and other complexities through your own shift in mindset.*
Bryan Timm, President and COO, Columbia Sportswear Company

Unite! *is the perfect antidote for the Peter Principle. The changes in behavior required for emerging leaders to succeed at senior levels are neither intuitive nor easy to make, and Sal has written an indispensable playbook for aspiring senior leaders and those invested in their success.*
Eric Roza, CEO, Datalogix and GM, Oracle Data Cloud

Great leadership is a critical component to scaling any fast-growing business, and finding senior leaders who can effectively lead the charge is not easy. Unite! *lays out the key distinctions to groom your people for senior leader roles and to help in your search as you look externally.*
Matt Warta, Co-founder and CEO, GutCheck

Unite! *helps senior leaders make subtle but important shifts in mindset to not only achieve tangible business results, but to connect more deeply with and build a winning mindset with their executives.*
Kane McCord, COO, Ibotta

Executive Coach Sal Silvester offers tools and insights into how you can successfully make the transition to senior leadership. This is a must read for those getting ready for promotion or looking to be more successful in senior leader roles.
Barbara Stevens, Chief Operating Officer, ReadyTalk

Author and management consultant Sal Silvester hits another homerun with his second leadership book, Unite! *Although I recommend reading* Ignite! *and* Unite! *in succession, this gem stands all on its own. It's a practical guide for any professional who is making the transition to a senior leadership role.*
Bob Allen, Director of Operations, City of Longmont, and Management Lecturer, University of Colorado, Boulder.

i

Making the transition into senior leadership comes with its own set of unique challenges. Unite! offers a pathway to help create your succession plans and build your senior leadership bench.
Michele Vion Choka, VP, Human Resources, Bill Barrett Corporation

With Unite!, *Sal Silvester is once again masterful in challenging and equipping leaders to better understand their personal leadership shadow.* Unite! *is a great resource guide for leaders to equip themselves to be inspirational, transformational, and to create a lasting legacy.*
Ettienne Bouwer, Director of Human Resources, Gallo Glass Company

The natural extension to Ignite!, *Sal shows us how his leadership teaching skills apply equally well to the realm of mountain rescue. And believe me, as a long-time valued member of one of the busiest search-and-rescue teams in the country, he gained these experiences in the real world.*
John Keller, Group Leader, Rocky Mountain Rescue Group, Boulder, Colorado

Unite! The 4 Mindset Shifts for Senior Leaders

By Sal Silvester

303-579-5829
sal@512solutions.com
http://www.512solutions.com

20660 Stevens Creek Blvd., Suite 210
Cupertino, CA 95014

Published by Happy About®
20660 Stevens Creek Blvd., Suite 210, Cupertino, CA 95014
http://happyabout.com

First Printing: May 2017
Paperback ISBN: 978-1-60005-269-9 (1-60005-269-X)
eBook ISBN: 978-1-60005-270-5 (1-60005-270-3)
Place of Publication: Silicon Valley, California, USA
Paperback Library of Congress Number: 2016963682

Trademarks

Warning and Disclaimer

Cover photo by Dave Christenson

Dedication

To the members of Rocky Mountain Rescue Group.

Also by Sal Silvester: *Ignite! The 4 Essential Rules for Emerging Leaders*

C o n t e n t s

x

Are you an emerging leader preparing for your next promotion into senior leadership? Maybe you're already a senior leader looking for additional tools to be more effective. Or perhaps you're an executive seeking new insights to help build your leadership bench.

For all you stars and rising stars alike, **Unite!** provides a practical model to help understand how senior leadership is different and the mindset shifts it takes to be successful. What's a mindset shift? It's an understanding of the beliefs and assumptions we have about ourselves and others that drive our current behaviors and identifying where those current beliefs are outdated, overused, and limiting our success. That's the work that I specialize in as an executive coach: helping already successful people uncover their limiting beliefs to drive sustainable change and success in the future.

This book isn't intended to be everything you need to know about senior leadership. It won't provide you with business and functional strategy or industry knowledge that you'll inevitably need in your role. That's not my area of expertise, and there are many other works that have addressed those topics. Instead, this book is intended purely with the focus on leadership behaviors.

The best teaching tool I know of is the learning parable. It's a story about a fictional person with real-life business and leadership challenges that illustrates all the essential elements of what you're trying to learn. Throughout the book, you'll get to know Ben Turner, the main character of the learning parable, and his colleagues as they navigate the complexities of senior leadership. Each chapter also contains related components of the Unite! Leadership Model.

This is the same model I use with my clients, and I want to share it with you.

People first,

Sal Silvester
January 2017
Boulder, Colorado

Ben Turner should have been whistling a happy tune.

Back when he worked for Stephanie in Professional Services, he had developed a reputation as the go-to technical guy at BCO-Tek. That solid reputation moved him up the ranks in lockstep promotion with Stephanie, who was now the president and CEO. Ben went from team leader in Professional Services to manager of several technical teams in Engineering. With his recent promotion to Vice President of Engineering, nearly 40 percent of the organization was reporting to his department. He now had more money and influence to help scale the fast-growing organization.

So why did everything feel like a struggle?

Making the transition into senior leadership is more complex than you think.

For many senior leaders, promotion is just the start of a whole new set of unexpected problems. Many for the first time are asked to work on multiple teams with peers who have competing priorities. They might now be responsible for areas of the organization in which they don't have technical expertise. And it's not just about the teams they lead anymore, because now there's a broader spectrum of constituents with which they have to engage.

In senior leadership, the complexity of the role increases and the consequences of a leader's behaviors are multiplied. How, then, can one successfully make the transition to senior leadership? What does it take to succeed at that level?

It takes, above all, four mindset shifts.

As the founder and president of two companies, 5.12 Solutions and Coachmetrix, I can tell you from years of experience coaching senior leaders and executives around the globe that making each of these four underlying **Mindset Shifts** is critical. These four **Mindset Shifts** are the focus of this book and the result of our work at 5.12 Solutions, including a survey we conducted of hundreds of people, from individual contributors to C-suite executives.

So that we have a common language on our journey together, first let me clarify how I distinguish among three general levels of leadership:

Emerging leaders: These are people who are in front-line to mid-level leadership roles. They are usually young, smart, and technically successful. They have such titles as supervisor, team leader, manager, and even senior manager.

Unite! The 4 Mindset Shifts for Senior Leaders

3

Senior Leaders: These are leaders with a significantly larger impact on an organization and have such titles as director, vice president, and senior vice president. They typically lead other leaders or run a functional area of an organization.

Executive Leaders: These leaders are generally at the enterprise level, often with profit and loss responsibilities. They have such titles as general manager and executive vice president and are related to the "C-suite."

These three levels are similar to what you'd see at small- or mid-sized organizations. In larger organizations, there are likely up to six levels of leadership to consider. Your role as you read this book is to customize the model to fit your situation.

More importantly, as you work through the **Unite! Leadership Model** in this book, you will find the tools, distinctions, and insights into how you can successfully transition into senior leadership. If you are already in a senior leadership role, you will find ways to improve how to function at that level with other senior leaders and on a leadership team. Our **Unite! Leadership Model** will also give you a framework to help coach leaders in the succession process to future senior leadership roles.

First, let's get back to Ben and see how he's coping.

1

To Tell the Truth . . . or Not

Kevin and Jen had an unspoken morning routine. They rolled their chairs to the edge of the imaginary boundary between their cubicles and peered out to the office entryway. This way, they could see what kind of mood their boss was in when he came through the door. Because on days when Ben Turner was in a bad mood, he became dogmatic and there was zero possibility of influencing his decisions. His five-foot-nine stature was not to be mistaken for being a pushover.

Kevin, lanky and with reddish-blond hair, had known Ben since the early days of BCO-Tek. Now Kevin was a senior manager on Ben's team. Jen wasn't quite as senior or nearly as organized, but she was a natural technician who could always be counted on.

On this particular morning, Kevin and Jen really needed to talk to Ben about an issue with Peter in Sales. Almost in unison, they pushed back to their cubicle boundary and peeked around the corner. They could see their boss making his way down the hallway toward them. The hunch of Ben's shoulders and the scowl on his face were unmistakable.

Unite! The 4 Mindset Shifts for Senior Leaders

5

"Not today," Kevin whispered to Jen.

She shook her head sadly. "No, not today," she agreed.

As Ben passed them, still focused on the screen of his mobile-friendly device, he asked them by rote, "Everything okay here?"

"Yup," Jen answered brightly, while Kevin shot him a thumbs-up.

The higher leaders rise, the more consequence there is to their actions. The first sign of trouble that they have lost touch with the basics: not hearing the truth from the people who work for them.

Unite! The 4 Mindset Shifts for Senior Leaders

7

Leaders need to know what's going on in order to run their functional area of the business effectively. The challenge is that as they rise in an organization, they also move further from the front lines of the business—whether it's the code being developed in a high-tech company or the customer in a retail company. They depend on their people to tell them what's what, but not everyone wants to step forward or be the bearer of bad tidings.

One of the ways in which senior leadership is more complex is that every behavior a leader exhibits or doesn't has a multiplier effect. People watch everything a leader does and does not do, especially when that leader isn't watching. They take their cue from there. We already know that positional power alone has an impact on whether a leader will hear what's truly going on in an organization. Throw in a bad mood or a strong personality, and that leader moves even further from hearing the truth.

It all goes back to the basics.

Even though the skillsets and mindsets required at senior-leader levels are more advanced, the basics still apply. When the basics aren't applied, there is a greater impact on people, process, and the business itself. In my book *Ignite! The 4 Essential Rules for Emerging Leaders*, I detailed the four practices of People-First Leadership™ that are the foundational components of leadership. These four essential rules are worth a quick review:

Lead by Example: This is the fundamental component of our People-First Leadership™ model outlined in *Ignite!* and will either establish or kill your credibility. Without it, you won't be able to move forward and build the credibility you need for success at senior leadership levels.

Align Your Team: Ultimately, aligning your team is about getting people to work on the right things. It starts by having a vision for your team and then clarifying goals and linking them to team and organizational priorities. The glue that holds it all together is providing coaching and feedback.

Build Cohesion: This is about getting people to work on the right things *together*. It's focusing on creating an environment of trust and respect through open communication, understanding style differences, and creating shared norms around how people work together. If aligning your team is about the "what" that needs to get done, building cohesion is the "how" those things get done.

Engage and Cultivate: Great leaders engage and cultivate their people by moving from a one-size-fits-all approach to building commitment by working with people at an individual level. Leaders learn to delegate effectively, create a motivating environment for their people, and create a recognition culture based on individual preferences.

While this book isn't about these four Rules, you need those basics in place before you're ready for the next step.

2 The Trouble with Sales

Darryl Remington always started Mondays the same way: walking around the office to check in with each of his team members. His agreeable tendencies and need to please others often left him in a position to not want to bother people, but back when Stephanie was mentoring him and Ben in their early days in Professional Services, Darryl learned to leverage his strength at creating process and structure to schedule "rounds," much like a nurse on a hospital floor. This helped to counteract his tendency toward avoidance.

After his morning rounds, Darryl sat at his desk and checked his emails. The one from Peter in Sales stood out: hiring was becoming an issue again. Darryl knew this to be true, but he wasn't yet willing to engage in what he thought would be another protracted battle.

With Darryl's recent promotion to Vice President of Product, he was responsible for both the product roadmap and marketing. On the product side, he was on solid footing, both as an engineer and through direct connection with customers when he was in the Professional Services department. He knew the product, he knew the industry, and he had a strong vision for the product's future. However, he lacked a marketing background. As he was also responsible for managing the marketing team and making sure the marketing efforts were in line with what customers wanted and needed, he often found himself caught between the Sales department's priorities and the Engineering department's capacity.

BCO-Tek, named after its hometown of Boulder, Colorado, started out as a software development shop in the garage of one of its founders. At first, they took on small web-based projects for local banks, but as they developed a product that helped financial institutions consolidate investment data for their customers, they grew to over $200 million in annual revenues and more than 350 employees. To create the physical space for that growth, the company had recently moved from downtown Boulder to a refurbished warehouse just east of downtown.

They were still ahead of the curve, having tapped early into the trend toward cloud-based solutions for smaller companies and leveraging their cash to hire young engineers and salespeople to help them move faster in the ever-changing tech and software-as-a-service industry. But in their race to stay ahead of the competition, BCO-Tek had a ton of hiring needs across the organization. There was an inevitable duel between hiring engineers to develop the software and hiring salespeople to sell it.

Tension was growing across the organization, and that was a natural phase of the organizational life cycle—or at least that's how Darryl rationalized it so he wouldn't have to deal with the issue head on.

It was hard to stay in this cocoon, though, especially now that Ben was walking briskly toward Darryl with a scowl on his face.

"Did you see that email yesterday from Peter in Sales?" Ben demanded.

"Good morning, sunshine," joked Darryl. Six-foot-one and lanky, Darryl was more laidback, but Ben and Peter both had strong personalities and were always jockeying for control. "Dude, I told you not to check your email on Sunday nights. I thought you went rock climbing this weekend. You love rock climbing. Couldn't you just enjoy it and give that prefrontal cortex a rest?"

"Peter's got a helluva nerve," said Ben, fuming. "He's asking for changes that just can't be done in such a short timeframe. We'll need at least ten more engineers, stat."

Darryl sighed to himself. Let the games begin, he thought.

An additional complexity
for senior leadership is
working with peers who have
competing priorities.

When my wife, Rachel, was pregnant with our first son, people kept telling us that "everything is going to change." Frankly, that unsolicited advice wasn't very helpful. What did it mean, really? Where were the action steps? My life has always been about action. In college, I partially paid for school through an ROTC scholarship and then went on active duty, jumping out of planes in Airborne School. I made my way through Ranger School and served overseas in Turkey and Kuwait. After four years on active duty, I landed a job with Accenture in management consulting. Now I run two businesses and volunteer on the Mountain Rescue Team in Boulder.

Action, baby!

For many senior leaders, it's the same (even if they don't jump out of planes). They understand that there will be a transition. They know they will have more responsibilities. But until they get some real action steps they can follow, just knowing things might be challenging in some vague, undefined way is not very helpful.

Before we explore the key mindset shifts needed to successfully transition into senior leadership, let's dive deeper into how senior leadership is different from the emerging-leader level.

More Complexity

The first component of what's going to change is simply the complexity of a senior leadership role. For the first time, many leaders who are accustomed to leading one team will be asked to work on multiple teams.

For example, they might lead the Human Resources function within the organization and also be on the CEO's leadership team. Or in Darryl and Ben's case, they lead the Product and Engineering departments, respectively, and are also on the CEO's leadership team. The challenge is that leaders are expected to be fully engaged members of the leadership team, yet they are usually rewarded based on the success of the function that they lead. Instead of being collaborative with their other highly successful peers, there's often tension and competition instead.

Adding to the complexity of senior leadership is the expanded scope of the role. A senior leader may run multiple teams, have to deal with cross-cultural issues, and be responsible for a more diverse workforce.

The real challenge behind all those surface issues is that that senior leaders often find themselves responsible for areas in which they may not have technical expertise. Here, Darryl's situation is not unusual: he has been incredibly successful leading a Product Management team and suddenly finds himself also responsible for Marketing.

Finally, there is a much broader spectrum of constituents with which senior leaders must engage. It's not all about the team they lead anymore. They often find themselves squeezed between the executives to whom they are accountable and the managers underneath who are looking for direction and coaching. Most often overlooked is the network of peers who become critically important to a senior leader's success. Did I already mention they likely have competing priorities?

Bigger Consequences

The second major way in which senior leadership is different is related to the consequence of these leaders' actions, inactions, and decisions. All eyes are suddenly upon you, and there's a multiplier effect based on what others see. That's what happened when Ben's bad mood translated into reluctance to speak up on the part of his direct reports.

The troops are watching. They're not missing a trick. Senior leaders mustn't underestimate the impact of what they do or do *not* do, what they say and do *not* say, how they reward and how they criticize. Their behaviors have significant consequences for people, process, and the organization. A senior leader recently told me that he was curious about the user interface a designer was creating. He simply asked a question about the rationale for one of the design changes. A week later, the entire interface had been redesigned based on the designer's assumptions about the senior leader's question. The positional power and impact that senior leaders have is powerful.

The consequences of a senior leader's actions are not only to others. There are also consequences to the senior leader's responsibilities. As mentioned in *The Leadership Pipeline* by Charon, Drotter, and Noel, in the past, senior leaders might have had a voice to "chime in on key decisions." Now, they may have full responsibility for those decisions. To make it even more complicated, these decisions often have to be made in the face of ambiguity and imperfect information.

Broader Consideration

The third major difference is what I call consideration—both for the near term and the future. Senior leaders not only have to direct the day-to-day aspects of the business, they also have to think longer term and more strategically about not just their own function but also the overall business. They have to develop skills to balance both the urgent and the important. Otherwise, the urgent will always rule their calendar.

3 The Downward Spiral

They were twenty minutes into an hour-long leadership team meeting, and it wasn't pretty.

"You're taking this personally, Ben," Peter said.

"I am NOT!" Ben insisted.

Stephanie had asked for this meeting. She learned early on that to develop a strong leadership team, the team needed to spend actual time together. At first, there was pushback to the idea of doing it weekly ("Enough meetings! When do we get to do REAL work?"), but Stephanie knew that getting the leadership team on better footing WAS the real work.

As usual, Darryl listened intently but didn't weigh in. Adrianna, the chief financial officer, and Mike, the chief human resources officer, pretty much checked out while Ben and Peter dug their heels in.

Peter used the phrase "head count," which Stephanie thought dehumanized people and negatively influenced how leaders made people-related decisions. "Bottom line, we need to create two additional Agile Development Teams in Engineering to meet the requirements Peter laid out in that email," Ben said.

Peter fought back. "That's another ten to twelve people, Ben! That's about twenty percent of our projected hiring for the next twelve months . . . for the entire organization!"

"If you want product for the customer, that's what it's going to take to hit your new goal."

Stephanie stepped in. "Darryl, we haven't heard from you," she said. "Technically, you're responsible for the product road map. What's your take?"

Darryl had dreaded this moment. He squinted his eyes. He looked to the left and the right, as if the correct response would magically materialize. By this time, thankfully, Ben and Peter were at it again.

"You're trying to hijack our entire organizational hiring plan," Peter accused.

"We're an engineering-driven organization," Ben shot back. "Period."

"Fine, then. We'll go with your plan," said Peter, not sounding fine with it at all.

Under stress, leaders can revert to their natural tendencies and derail their own efforts.

Unite! The 4 Mindset Shifts for Senior Leaders

19

Under stress, senior leaders tend to lean toward an overly results-oriented style or an overly relationship-oriented style. When these two styles are out of balance, the downside is massive.

Before we can get into four critical mindset shifts that senior leaders need to make to be successful, we have to understand two important dimensions that can help us uncover what drives our current mindsets and can give leaders insight into what they need to do to become more effective. These two dimensions help explain what makes great senior leaders great:

Results and Relationships

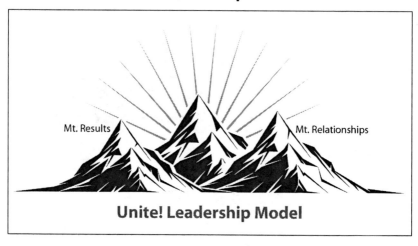

Unite! Leadership Model

RESULTS are what the corporate workplace usually reward. Get the job done. Accomplish goals. Meet your objectives and key results. Achieve your MBOs. Track your KPIs. This is what executive leaders generally value, and for good reason. Organizational shareholders and stakeholders want to see their leaders creating value. Results, as defined in this book, is the achievement of our performance indicators.

RELATIONSHIPS: The second dimension of great senior leadership is Relationships, commonly defined by how effectively leaders engage with others. Relationships come from their ability to communicate and collaborate, to create a positive work environment, and to generate commitment from the people around them as they deal with the complexity of workplace issues. This "softer" side of leadership is commonly ignored because it isn't as easily measured as Results. But within this dimension are hidden elements that can bring success or can completely derail a senior leader's career.

The Unbalanced Leader

Many of us are naturally inclined to lean toward one or the other of these two dimensions. That is, we tend to be overly focused on results or overly focused on relationships.

Take Ben, for example. His fast-paced results orientation has made him a successful and highly respected leader. But his desire to get results is so strong that he often interrupts, overrules, and plows over others. Some consider Ben arrogant—the classic overuse of confidence. What makes it difficult for Ben to change is that these behavioral tendencies have helped him be successful in the past, so he equates them with what will help him be successful in the future at the senior-leadership level. The unfortunate part of his style is that he gets results at the expense of others. He leaves dead bodies in his wake.

When one of these two tendencies strongly outweighs the other, there's a cost—either to the organization or to the people who you lead. Ben is likely to get the outcome he wants or needs, but only in the short term. He does it in a way that generates compliance, not commitment. People are likely to do what he tells them to do, but not because of an internal motivational driver or because of dedication to Ben; they simply comply because it's easier. Their desire is to avoid pain.

But let's not just pick on the overly results-driven leader, because there is also a cost to being overly focused on relationships over results. Like Ben, Darryl is well respected by his people and by the executive leaders above him. He's friendly, approachable, and collaborative in nature. He listens, reflects, and asks good questions. At times, he even challenges others—except when the situation gets uncomfortable. Because of his agreeable nature and strong underlying need to please, he tends to focus on the relationships he has with others and avoids having difficult conversations. He fails to consistently create a culture of accountability and straight talk, where he and his people can go directly to each other when there are issues. When leaders avoid critical conversations or holding others accountable, they lose credibility. Worse, their teams tend to focus on the wrong things or good people leave because they see others being rewarded for behaviors that don't warrant it.

The Balanced Leader

The bottom line is that great leaders need to balance both results and relationships. To truly unite the people around them, they must focus *both* on driving results for the organization while maintaining and building relationships with others.

Do not mistake this for lowered standards. We are not asking Ben to lessen his focus on results or Darryl to be careless about his relationships. Quite the contrary! Ben and Darryl, like all senior leaders, need to maintain their strengths while cultivating their opposing tendencies.

4 Mindset What?

"You and Peter went at it pretty hard the other day, Ben," Stephanie noted at the Product/Engineering meeting she held every two weeks for Ben and Darryl.

Ben was unapologetic. *"We have some serious Engineering needs if we want to meet Peter's sales goals,"* he said.

Darryl entered in a blaze, apologizing right and left. *"Sorry I'm late, my last meeting went over,"* he said. *"What did I miss?"*

"Gentlemen, we start on time," Stephanie said. *"Our agreement is clear."* She had worked hard to curtail the unspoken *"late but not too late"* norm that had been rampant in the organization, although it still happened from time to time. Meetings used to start about seven minutes late. The key was not to be the last person in the room, so as not to embarrass yourself, and not to be the first, so as to not waste your time, but in a three-person meeting, you were either on time or not.

"We were just doing a debrief on the leadership-team meeting the other day," said Stephanie.

"Uh, yeah," said Darryl. *"Good times."*

"I didn't hear much from you," said Ben.

Darryl shrugged off the implication, not wanting to stoke the unspoken conflict that was obviously brewing between Ben and Peter.

"What was your intent in that meeting, Ben?" asked Stephanie.

"To make sure that Engineering's perspective was considered," said Ben.

"And what do you think the outcome was?"

"That Peter heard what I had to say."

"We all heard you, Ben," said Stephanie. "But how committed do you think Peter will be based on your approach?"

"Oh, he's pretty committed," said Ben. "He said he'd go with my plan."

Stephanie turned to Darryl and asked for his thoughts on that.

"Um, it was kinda rough that day," said Darryl. "You definitely won the argument, Ben, but you might have left a dead body or two in your wake."

Stephanie drew three concentric circles on her whiteboard. Inside the smallest one in the center, she wrote "Intentions." On the middle circle, she wrote "Behaviors." On the outer circle, she wrote "Perceptions."

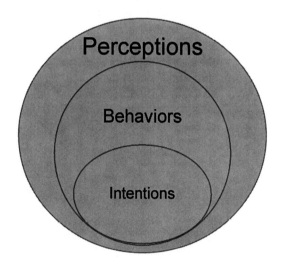

"Intentions, that's pretty self-explanatory," she said. *"That what you intend to do or say, and these intentions often go unspoken. Behaviors, here in the middle, are what other people observe. The largest circle is Perceptions, which are the conclusions people come to based on your behaviors. See?"*

Darryl nodded, although he wasn't sure what he was seeing. Ben appeared to be studying the diagram.

"When your intentions and behaviors aren't aligned, the perceptions others have of you won't be aligned either," Stephanie explained. *"The result is unnecessary conflict and lack of commitment."*

"But he said he'd go along with my plan!" Ben blurted out.

"He might," said Stephanie. *"But I don't believe you won Peter's commitment. I think your intent was solid. What you said was fine, but how you said it, with an overly aggressive approach, may create perceptions that you are closed-minded or even autocratic. Your peers are highly successful people and generally won't respond well to that type of approach."*

"Huh," said Ben. *"I hadn't considered that." Ben had been working to minimize his tendency to be defensive, and thought he had it licked.*

"How about you, Darryl?" said Stephanie. *"What perceptions might people conclude from your behaviors in that meeting?"*

"Me?" Darryl said with a gulp. "Uh, well, I was pretty quiet, I guess," he said. *"I was just trying to take everything in because I can understand both perspectives."*

"Again, good intentions," said Stephanie. *"By being quiet, though, you might have come across as overly passive and as a result, disengaged. The rest of the leadership team, not just Peter and Ben, need to hear your perspective too."*

When a leader's intentions are not aligned with behavior, the perception can derail a career.

The Peter Principle, first formulated by Laurence J. Peter, predicts that you will get promoted up to your level of incompetence. For most senior leaders, that's far too late. Because when leaders get promoted to their level of incompetence, they lose their confidence. They become stuck. Worse, they make incompetent decisions that others in the organization are forced to live with.

The bottom line is that what derails most leaders at senior leadership levels has less to do with skillsets and more to do with underlying behavioral tendencies of which the leader might not be aware. As a result of these tendencies, the perceptions others have of their leaders are often misaligned with a leaders' intentions. In the senior leadership world where there is more complexity, consequence, and consideration, there's too much at stake to risk this misalignment.

There are four common and costly career behaviors that derail senior leaders like Ben and Darryl.

Leaders like Ben who are overly focused on results and don't emphasize relationships enough tend to derail themselves though the following behaviors:

Controlling: This strong autocratic tendency to control one's environment, speak up about problems, and challenge the system can be extremely positive. At its worst, though, it can lead to such negative outcomes as a lack of delegation. The big issue with this at senior levels is not just the lack of handing over a task but also the inability to scale a business and operate at the right level. The collateral damage to the people around these leaders includes not feeling valued and trusted, which eventually leads to disengagement.

Arrogance is a tendency when overly results-oriented leaders overuse their strength of confidence. People experience this behavior as egocentric and superior, and this destructive tendency shuts down conversation and innovation (after all, the arrogant leader already knows the answer!) and can ruin relationships. For example, we recently coached an executive and co-founder of a fast-growing high-tech company. His leading questions often steered people to his pre-formed conclusions instead of opening a space for input from others. Arrogance perpetuates a win-lose orientation, where the arrogant leader feels a need to come out on top. The danger, of course, is that the outcome of these pre-decided decisions may compromise the business.

Then there are leaders like Darryl, who are overly focused on relationships and not enough on results. They risk experiencing these career derailers:

Passivity is when leaders don't voice their perspective and too often defer to others. They justify this tendency with statements like, "I only want to speak when I have something meaningful to say." I see this tendency most in humble leaders, people who don't need to be in the spotlight. That is refreshing in small doses, but its overuse makes those leaders seem like rollovers, people who don't control or lead, who don't step up or know what they've accomplished. They miss opportunities. Overly passive leaders don't instill confidence in their peers or in the executives above them.

Avoidance is similar to passivity, but it's mostly about how a leader responds in conflict. At senior-leader levels, leaders have to be willing to take risks and put their perspective on the line. In many ways, it's a vulnerable behavioral set. Sometimes those risks are in accountability conversations. Other times it's when they need to step up to provide a perspective. That's what they are paid to do. But with this tendency, they prefer to avoid those conversations, and they fail to hold people to the high standards that are necessary for moving the business forward.

It doesn't have to be this way, either for people like Ben or like Darryl. I know through my experience coaching leaders with these strong tendencies that they can change. Some of the latest research about the brain confirms it: you *can* teach an old dog new tricks. The brain's neurons are flexible, and people can learn new ways of behaving at all ages and experience levels.

To change your perceptions, you cannot simply change a few behaviors. You have to go deeper. You have to change your *intention*, which requires a mindset shift.

It's a Mindset Shift

As leaders transition into more senior roles and they encounter resistance and conflict due to misalignments of their intentions, behaviors, and perceptions, they often look to improve their skills. They look at successful and unsuccessful leaders above and around them for clues. They often seek a laundry list of "success" characteristics that they can adopt.

Those proactive steps are important but not sufficient. The exercise usually yields surface-level observations while failing to identify the underlying beliefs that need to shift at the senior-leader level.

Don't get me wrong—the transition into senior leadership *does* require new skillsets. We already know that leading at higher levels is more complex. There is more consequence to a leader's actions, and the leader has to consider both near-term and long-term perspectives. However, as I've noticed through years of working with leadership teams, in 1-1 executive coaching sessions and in long-term leadership development programs, *the transition into senior leadership is less about the skills a leader needs to develop and mostly about the mindset changes a leader needs to shift.* Understand these mindset shifts, and you'll likely be on an accelerated path to success.

What is a mindset shift? It is a change in a belief or assumption you already have. It is also the creation of a new positive belief about something you do not currently embrace.

The mistake most leaders make is that they think about something they want to change—a new result they want to have—and they immediately go into action mode to get it. The missing critical component is to examine the ingrained mindset they already have, because the mindset is usually the driver of our actions. A positive mindset results in a series of actions that lead you toward what you want. With a limiting mindset, you will follow a series of actions that actually *decrease* your ability to reach your goal.

Understanding one's mindset is the deeper issue we need to address before we can make sustainable change, whether it has to do with leadership development or any other area of our lives.

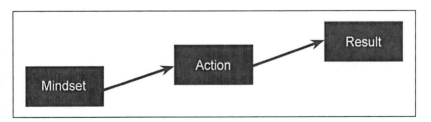

An example is the boy who grows up in a household where fitness isn't valued. It is not only not valued, it is criticized. When athletes appear on TV or neighbors run by the house, the boy hears snide comments from his parents about the spandex clothing or how slowly the person is running. Fast forward to the beginning of freshman year in high school, where the boy starts hanging out with people who are physically fit. He realizes that he has put on weight and needs to do something about it—especially with the upcoming homecoming celebration. He sets a goal to lose ten pounds by the middle of the term and begins to run track after school each day. But he has this nagging vibe in his head. He slogs through exercise but hates every minute of it and in the end, doesn't get many results after all. A boy in this situation almost inevitably develops a negative belief system around health and fitness, and it unwittingly gets in the way of his living a vibrant and healthy life. Before he can successfully embrace fitness and sustainably lose ten pounds, he'll have to change how he thinks about fitness by building awareness of his limiting mindset and how it developed. Until then, he'll be less likely to create sustainable change around his weight loss.

When it comes to senior leadership, skills are critical. Skills, in a way, are a "pay to play" requirement in almost any leadership role. In other words, without the technical competency to do your role, you won't be qualified and respected as a leader, period.

But senior leaders cannot get by on technical skills alone. It's ultimately the mindset shifts that can enable these leaders to overcome the common and costly career derailers that so easily bring them down.

In the upcoming chapters, we will explore the Four Key Mindset Shifts that are critical to navigating the changes that come with senior leadership.

Mindset Shift 1

5 Mindset Shift 1 – From Smart to Aware

Ben got to work immediately. Even though he had won the argument with Peter in Stephanie's leadership team meeting, he knew he had to prove that his hiring plan was better than Peter's—that it was more "aligned" with what the organization needed at this moment. After all, without engineers, BCO-Tek wouldn't have product.

Ben gathered data about software releases from the previous six months, being sure to directly link the cost of hiring new engineers with how the products were received by BCO-Tek's customers. Jen and Kevin helped gather additional information to help Ben make his case on paper.

That afternoon, Ben went over to Darryl to get his input too. "Hey, take a look," he said, handing Darryl a summary of the plan he intended to share with Stephanie later that day in the standing Product and Engineering meeting. "My team has done our assessment, and I've confirmed we'll need two additional agile development teams to meet the needs of Peter's sales plan and of our customers."

Darryl looked over the plan. "Hmm, seems aggressive," he said. Then he added, "Cool. We're kinda behind on our mobile offering and that's a key product strategy in the next six months."

"So, you'll back me in the meeting today?" Ben confirmed.

"Umm, what do you mean? Uh, sure," said Darryl.

"Great!" That's all Ben needed to validate his perspective. He couldn't wait for the afternoon meeting.

Senior leadership isn't about being smart—it's about being aware.

The Shift

In a survey we conducted on senior leadership, we asked senior leaders the following question: "What do you wish you knew more about senior leadership prior to being promoted to a senior leader role?"

Overwhelmingly, senior leaders responded with themes around understanding their own emotions and being more empathetic and not reactive during conflict.

This leads to the first mindset shift in our Unite! Leadership Model required to successfully navigate the transition into senior leadership: the move from being *Smart* to being *Aware*.

I call this enhanced state of awareness, *Interpersonal Agility*.

At the emerging-leader level, you were likely a technical expert, and that's what got you promoted. You were good at what you did, so someone said, "Let's promote this person!" Even though you might have recognized the need to get work done through others, you could still get away with overcoming organizational challenges by falling back on being the technical expert. Your technical skills and smarts trumped the need to actually lead.

At the senior-leader level, this no longer works.

This is primarily because of the challenges of senior leadership roles that we explored previously—the complexity of the role, the consequence of your decisions, and consideration for both the short- and long-term issues.

At senior leadership levels, you now have a much broader spectrum of stakeholders with whom to engage—the executive leaders you work for, the extensive network of peers with whom you have to negotiate resources, and the people who work for you. The technical knowledge and skills that made you successful in the past do not arm you with the tools you need to manage your emotions in the midst of the chaos and complexity that comes with senior leadership. If you don't make the shift from trying to be *Smart* to being *Aware*, you won't be equipped to stay engaged in the dialogue that it takes to negotiate with others who have competing priorities, and to make well-intended decisions with the organization in mind. You'll be caught up instead in the swirl of conflict and damaged relationships, as silos build across functional areas of the business.

Let's distinguish between being *Smart* and being *Aware*.

Being *smart* is about proving your worth, about demonstrating to others that you are the technical expert. There's nothing inherently wrong with this orientation, except that it's not scalable. "Smart" leaders tend to be less conscious of the impact they have on people, process, and the business.

"Aware" leaders, on the other hand, ultimately have a deeper understanding of themselves and of their impact on others. It's an understanding of the wake they leave behind when they lead others.

Aware leaders understand the following:

- Why do others respond to you the way they do?
- Why do you respond to others the way you do?
- What in your environment is triggering the reaction you are currently experiencing?

For some, it may be building awareness of their defensiveness or recognizing their over-passivity in meetings. Perhaps it's seeing how arrogant they come across based on the body language and facial expressions they unwittingly project.

You can identify leaders who fail to make the shift from *Smart* to *Aware* by looking for the following:

- They typically start discussions by advocating for their own position.
- When another team member suggests an alternative, smart but unaware leaders get defensive, argumentative, or withdrawn, signaled by a quick response to negate the other's opinion or idea.
- They have difficulty not taking things personally and aren't aware of how their body language and style affect their team members.
- They might be able to see their own dysfunctional behavior after the meeting is over or the interaction is complete, but they miss seeing it in real time, when they could have done something about it.

- They have a difficult time understanding the needs of other senior leaders and empathizing with competing sets of priorities. As a result, they justify their silo-building behaviors of withholding information, being aggressive, or unnecessarily remaining in conflict.

It's all a downward spiral from there.

On the other hand, it's also easy to identify leaders who make the shift from *Smart* to *Aware* because you'll notice the following:

- They have the ability to engage in dialogue and debate in a constructive manner without taking disagreement personally.

- They don't shy away from difficult conversations, and they remain open in the process.

- They maintain an openness to advocate for their point of view while simultaneously considering the points of view of others.

- They treat others as human beings—people with different pressures and priorities that come with running their own functional areas of the business.

When you begin to develop this sense of awareness, you remain composed in the midst of stressful situations and continue to move interactions forward to a more positive outcome.

6 The Self-Observer

Ben and Darryl were back at it again with Stephanie. It seemed that their regular Product/Engineering meetings had turned into the old mentor/coaching sessions Stephanie had run with them when they were transitioning into their first emerging-leader roles.

"Ben, what did you notice when you met with Peter this week?" Stephanie asked.

"It was a pretty intense conversation," said Ben. "Peter and I have different perspectives."

"I'm asking for something more specific," said Stephanie. "Do you notice anything about your body during these intense conversations?"

"I know!" Darryl jumped in. "My face gets flushed, my field of vision narrows, and I feel pressure in my head."

"Good observation," Stephanie said. "Ben?"

"I see what you mean," said Ben. "I can literally feel it in my chest. My heartbeat intensifies, and I noticed that I tend to squint. Maybe more like a scowl. Maybe that's why people say I'm intimidating."

"It hits me in the gut," said Darryl.

"That's where the term 'gut feeling' comes in," Stephanie agreed. "So, guys, based on how you each responded in the moment, would you work for you? Would you want yourself as your boss?

Ben scowled, and Darryl picked at a thread on his jacket.

"Think of these physiological changes as an alarm that triggers you to try something different," said Stephanie. "The next time you notice these changes, take specific steps to reflect, breathe, and then do something different than you normally do so that you can remain in a productive conversation with others. I call it the self-observer's model. Here's how it works . . ."

There are tools you can use to start building awareness.

Unite! The 4 Mindset Shifts for Senior Leaders

41

Here are two tools to help you build self-awareness and better understand the impact you have on others.

Tool #1: The Self-Observer

The first tool is a three-step process to enable you to better see your impact on others. We call it the "self-observer." The intent of this tool is to help you observe the wake that you leave behind as you lead others, and to understand the perceptions others glean from your behaviors. It's also about understanding why you react to others the way that you do.

Self-aware leaders can literally step outside themselves and view what they are doing and saying, as if they are watching a video in real time through the eyes of an objective observer. These leaders are able to clearly hear the words they use, assess the tonality of their voice, and observe their body language. Most people can reflect back after an interaction and recognize some of those key components—words, tonality, and body language—but the key to being a successfully self-aware leader is being able to do this in the moment and make adjustments so as to stay in conversation.

Step 1: Listen to your body. What do you physically notice about your body in conflict? Do you tense up? Does your face get hot? How does your gut feel? Start building awareness of the physiological changes that happen in your body during stress or an intense conversation. At first, just observe these changes; later, these will serve as triggers to alert you to take different action.

Step 2: Change your state. This step is designed to get you out of the psychological state that you are in so that you can remain in conversation with others. In the workplace, this might be about reflecting before responding or creating space or time before responding. You might first ask a question to seek clarification or understanding, instead of just reacting. You might paraphrase what you heard. In a sense, it's like a broadcast delay that happens on radio. That's when they intentionally delay the broadcast of live material for a few seconds in case they need to bleep out profanity, bloopers, or other embarrassing mistakes. Usually that's all we need in the workplace too—just a few seconds in which to make a different choice about how to respond to a situation. We can create such a delay simply by saying, "Tell me more." It gives us time to be the self-observer and make a better choice in how to respond.

Step 3: Make a choice. Choice is the ability to maintain composure in the face of stress and complexity so you can make the most of your interactions with others. Truly effective leaders are able to make a choice about the words they use, the tonality of their voice, or the body language they project. During this step, keep in mind that other leaders in your organization, mostly peers who run other functions, are human beings too, all with their own goals, challenges, and pressures. According to the Arbinger Institute, when we don't see people as people and instead see them as objects, we tend to marginalize them in the workplace. From there, our thinking gets distorted, and we begin to justify our less-than-productive behaviors.

For example, take Eric, the division president for a global Fortune 100 company. We observed him during a meeting with two of his trusted team members as they brainstormed about a potential new product offering. We noticed Eric in his interactions with one of the team members literally shoot down every idea that member had. It started almost immediately as the meeting began, even during an informal ice-breaking conversation. It then permeated every relevant business discussion that followed over the next hour. When we asked Eric about it later, he justified his behavior through a distorted lens: "That's just me. I challenge everyone's ideas." When we asked the team member about the impact these interactions had on him, he said, "I lost an entire night's sleep over this one-hour meeting. I took a hit to my confidence, felt completely incompetent, and noticed that I withdrew from the conversation."

Eric was blind to the impact his behavior had on this talented team member. By not seeing that team member as a human being, he risks losing out on the best work that this talented individual can provide.

Being a vigilant and consistent self-observer enables a new level of self-awareness. Moving to this higher state of being sets the foundation for everything that senior leaders have to do as they deal with the added complexity, consequence, and consideration associated with their roles. Leaders who do not make this shift will never achieve their potential with the remaining three mindset shifts either.

Tool #2: Seek Feedback

Feedback is one of the most effective ways to help create awareness and behavioral change, and it can happen formally or informally. Either way, it adds a level of discipline and structure to behavioral change that most people simply don't employ.

Here are three ideas for gathering feedback:

1. *The verbal Likert scale.* Simply ask for feedback by saying something like, "Hey Jim, I've been working on being more assertive in sharing my perspective in meetings. On a scale of one to five, where one is low assertiveness and five is high assertiveness, how did I just do in that leadership team meeting?" Forcing the other person to give a number then gives you a jumping-off point for gathering more details. Jim may respond with, "I'd give you a three out of five," to which your response could be, "Great, thank you. And what would I need to do to get closer to a four or five?" This entire process takes less than a minute, and not only helps you get a real-time read, it also advertises to others that you are still working on creating personal change.

2. *The half-time adjustment.* This is a process that works well in a group setting and that can give you valuable feedback for making adjustments. Conduct the following process about a third or halfway into the meeting. It will take only a minute to complete and will give valuable information that can make a significant difference in how you conduct the remainder of the meeting.

   - Pause or stop the group.

   - Facilitate a quick discussion on things that are going well so far in the meeting (pluses).

   - Facilitate a quick discussion on what to stop or do differently to make the meeting more effective (deltas).

   - Document your findings on a whiteboard or flip chart.

3. *360 Feedback.* This is a more formal feedback process that we utilize in our executive coaching and leadership development engagements. The process entails an online assessment that gathers 360 feedback from a leader's direct reports, as well as from peers, managers, and others, to help leaders understand how they are perceived by the people they work with on a regular basis. For more intensive execu-

tive coaching engagements, we conduct confidential one-on-one interviews to gather similar 360 feedback, so leaders better understand their impact on others.

Coachmetrix™ Now we have created a new and innovative tool that leaders can use to create self-awareness and improve their interpersonal agility. It's called **Coachmetrix** and has already been used with hundreds of leaders across the country.

We use **Coachmetrix** in our leadership development and coaching engagements—and you can, too, to help facilitate and optimize your programs. It's a cloud-based system that we developed and now offer to other coaches, trainers, and leaders through a subscription service (see www.coachmetrix.com for more information). **Coachmetrix** optimizes the coaching experience by measuring behavior change through a pulse feedback mechanism. It effectively automates the verbal Likert Scale method mentioned above, so leaders can see their patterns of perceived behavior over time. **Coachmetrix** also includes a self-assessment as part of the pulse feedback process so leaders can quickly identify where there are gaps in how they see themselves and how others perceive them. **Coachmetrix's** action planning and discussion features also enable transparency between the Coach/Leader and Participant. And the system is robust enough to completely replace your performance management system with a more agile process that provides people with ongoing feedback instead of feedback just a few times during the year.

Feedback is a critical method for making the shift from *Smart* to *Aware* because there is always a lag between when a leader makes a change and when others perceive that change. And leaders don't get to stop working on something just because they think others will see the change they made. They only get to stop working on something when others tell them they've seen the change.

7 | Emotional IQ on the Mountain

Ben was a long-time member of the Rocky Mountain Rescue Group, one of the oldest and most prestigious mountain rescue teams in the country. The team had already hiked up almost two thousand vertical feet through the windy drainage, ascending from the base of Chautauqua Park in Boulder up a steep gulley between the first and second Flatirons. The nearly vertical layers of rock extend in some cases over 800 feet high and are layered on top of the Boulder foothills. It marks the entranceway into the steeper and taller Rocky Mountain range and is a sight so stunning that it has long been symbolic of Boulder.

The team often had to solve complex rescue scenarios involving injured climbers or hikers in awkward and unforgiving terrain. Ben's engineering mindset suited him well for this kind of work.

Today, the team was responding to a practice scenario, as they did just about every other Sunday morning to keep their rescue skills sharp. For Ben, this was an especially important moment, as he was working hard to achieve the next level of rescue title in the hierarchy, where he would have even more responsibility on missions and lead even more people. Unlike in an office environment, the decisions Ben made on a mountaintop would have significant impact on the safety of all around him—the patient, his fellow rescuers, and any bystanders that were often in the area.

As site lead, the senior leader who was responsible for organizing the initial stages of the rescue at the patient location, there was a lot to do. In this particular case, the scenario called for the team to move quickly, as the patient was considered "trauma red."

Ben went running up to the "practice" patient and began barking orders to his teammates. "John, take medical. Chris, Steve, Lisa, you're on the litter"—the reinforced rescue stretcher used to carry patients out of the backcountry—"Paul, build an anchor," which was a system that would support the litter team as they were lowered down the steep terrain.

The team worked quickly. There was a massive sense of urgency. Ben popped over to the litter and helped the team put the two litter pieces together. Then he ran over to the anchor and without saying anything, began to help Paul. "I've got it, Ben," Paul said.

The mood intensified. As Ben continued to bark orders, others spoke louder and moved faster.

"Stop," called John, the group leader. He was in charge of the day's practice and of using real-time opportunities for the team to pause and learn in the moment. Almost everyone was in a "stretch" role today, not just Ben. "Okay, what are you noticing?" John asked. He didn't bias the group with a leading question, even though he obviously had his reasons for stopping the action at that point.

Team members began to chime in. They were moving quickly, maybe too much so. They had the right gear in place. John used a debrief method he had learned in the workplace that involved three simple questions: What happened? So what? Now what? The intent was to help people understand the cause and effect of their behaviors.

"Ben, you were the site lead," said one of the team members. "I noticed that the more intensity you brought to the situation, the more everyone else's energy level rose."

"So what?" said John, probing deeper. "Why is that important for Ben to know?"

"We're all looking up to the senior person, so there's a tendency for us to do what you do," said the team member. "It's good to some extent because it creates urgency, but here, we shifted from moving with a calm assertiveness to acting chaotically. That means we're at risk of making mistakes."

Higher levels of awareness lead to more effective business results.

Of the four mindset shifts, the shift from *Smart* to *Aware* is the most important. Leaders typically obtain their jobs because of their technical knowledge, but they become successful in these roles because of their ability to understand their impact to others. With that deeper level of understanding, they are better able to nurture and maintain professional relationships and make better decisions on behalf of the business.

Making the shift from *Smart* to *Aware* is ultimately about elevating one's emotional intelligence, a term that was popularized by Dan Goleman in his 1996 book of the same name. We define Emotional Intelligence as the ability to recognize, understand, and adapt your emotions so you can maintain and enhance interpersonal relationships.

The following is some incredibly compelling research on the subject.

According to the book *EI 2.0* by Travis Bradberry and Jean Greaves, when they compared star performers with average ones in senior leadership positions, nearly 90 percent of the differences in their profiles was attributable to emotional intelligence factors rather than cognitive abilities. They went on to say:

• Self-awareness is so important for job performance that 83 percent of people high in self-awareness are top performers, while just 2 percent of bottom performers are high in self-awareness.

• When you are self-aware, you are far more likely to pursue the right opportunities, put your strengths to work, and perhaps most importantly, keep your emotions from holding you back.

Clearly, if you hope to successfully navigate the complexity, consequence, and consideration that comes with senior leadership, you will need to make the shift from *Smart* to *Aware*. Your intellect and other innate characteristics will get you TO the role, but your ability to be self-aware and respond effectively in the moment will make you successful IN the role.

Reflection Questions – Mindset Shift 1: From Smart to Aware

To build awareness and start to make the shift, reflect on the following questions:

- What are your key strengths?
- What are your weaknesses?
- What are your blind spots (weaknesses you may not know about)?
- Where do your natural tendencies lie?
  - Does your strong need to seek the approval of others steer your behavior?
  - Does controlling others or your environment drive you?
  - Do you seek safety by remaining distant?
- Why do you respond to others the way you do (especially with personalities that are more difficult for you to navigate)?
- Why do others respond to you the way they do?
- Where are your intentions and behaviors aligned with the perceptions others have of you?
- Where are your intentions and behaviors misaligned with the perceptions others have of you?
- What underlying mindsets drive your behavior (both positive and negative)?
- What physiological factors show up when you are in difficult conversations?
- What questions or phrases can you use to create space between another person's statement and your reaction to it?
- Where are there opportunities for you to seek feedback from others?

Unite! The 4 Mindset Shifts for Senior Leaders

51

Mindset Shift 2

Unite! The 4 Mindset Shifts for Senior Leaders

53

8 Mindset Shift 2 – From a Problem Orientation to an Outcome Orientation

Darryl could see that his people needed help. Years ago, he would have jumped in and just fixed the issue—not so much because he wanted to control his environment, the way Ben did, but because he didn't want to impose on his people by adding more to their plate. He used to "feel guilty" for delegating more work to them. After all, they were overloaded too.

This was no longer the case. Darryl now understood that he couldn't help scale the business if he held onto everything.

He walked over to a team member's desk to get the lay of the land on what was causing the current problem. It was becoming clear that a competitor's product had key features that were resonating with the market. But the real urgency among Darryl's people was that this competitor was well funded and scrappy. The competitor could move faster and pivot without the process requirements that BCO-Tek had put in place now that it had grown.

To handle the situation, Darryl called a meeting. He included Peter and a few other members of the US Sales team. He also invited Ben, as Engineering would be the ones to implement any solution.

The meeting went smoothly. Ben stood out in particular, as he had begun to make significant changes as a result of Stephanie's coaching in the Product-Engineering meetings. It didn't come naturally to him, but Ben was now advocating for his own positions while remaining open to what other people had to say too. At times, he slipped, but because he let Darryl and Peter know about the changes he was trying to make, they gave him the benefit of the doubt.

Darryl knew Ben was working hard on the change. He also knew Peter was a little skeptical. But for now, things were good.

"This is a critical product fix for you, Peter. Tell me why," Ben said.

"It opens up more of the US market for us," Peter replied. "It's a core feature in most of the new competitors entering this space, and our customers are asking for it."

"Ben, how quickly do you think you could roll this out?" asked Darryl.

"It's a month's worth of work," replied Ben. "But if we de-prioritize some of the other features, we can roll it out in the next two-week sprint. Can you guys live with that?" The "sprint" is a set period of time in which software engineers code a specific scope of work and roll it out to the market.

"Let's do it," Darryl said, more decisively than usual. "Ben, you and I can talk later about which features we'll postpone to a later sprint."

Everyone packed up and left, quite satisfied that they were moving in the right direction.

But were they?

Senior leaders often fall into the trap of solving one problem at a time.

Unite! The 4 Mindset Shifts for Senior Leaders

57

The Shift

The second mindset shift in our Unite! Leadership Model that senior leaders need to make is a shift from a *Problem Orientation* to an *Outcome Orientation*.

We've found through surveys and our work with clients that at the emerging-leader level (e.g., supervisors, managers), people typically approach their work with a problem orientation. In other words, they see a problem and they fix it. They see another problem and they fix that one too. It's a never-ending process of tension and relief as problems arise and the leader fixes them. The leader, usually without knowing it, has a dysfunctional belief that leadership is about rescuing others instead of teaching, delegating, and coaching. They are able to conceal their leadership weaknesses with their technical skills—and usually very successfully!

When senior leaders operate this way, they end up working on the wrong things. As a result, they force all the leaders beneath them to work at lower levels too. In *The Leadership Pipeline* by Ram Charan, Steve Drotter, and Jim Noel, they call this clogging up the leadership pipeline. Unfortunately, that's not a scalable model for fast-growing companies.

We asked executive leaders (e.g., C-suite leaders), "What is the biggest mistakes you see senior leaders (e.g., Vice Presidents, Directors) making?" Two themes arose in their answers: (1) lack of vision and (2) failure to hire the right people. The answer was similar when we asked team members (those who work for the senior leader) a similar question, "What is the biggest mistake your senior leaders make?" In their responses, they wanted to know more about the big picture—the mission, vision, goals, expectations, and success factors.

The shift from a *Problem Orientation* to an *Outcome Orientation* requires senior leaders to broaden their perspective and take a more systems approach so they operate at the right level. It's an approach that requires leaders to (1) think beyond their own functional area, (2) consider a longer-term view, and (3) build people capacity.

9 Cross-Organizational Advocacy

Usually Ben was in the hot seat in the meetings with Stephanie, but now it was Darryl's turn, and Ben was enjoying it.

"We're butting up against compression in our market," Stephanie said. "There are some quality start-ups that are offering similar services with a reasonable amount of quality and price pressure. What are you noticing, Darryl?"

Darryl glanced quickly at Ben before responding. "I feel like we are being reactive, and that's different than being agile," he said.

"Good awareness, Darryl," Stephanie said as she went to the whiteboard. "You can think about leadership in terms of three mountain peaks. There's Mount Results and Mount Relationships, and the goal is not to get stuck for too long on either of those peaks. From there, you can't get where you want to go, which is the higher peak in the middle. That's where you find superb leadership."

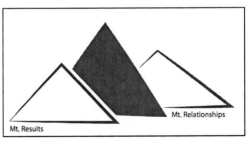

She drew three triangles on the whiteboard to resemble three peaks. The one in the middle was the tallest. "Your first Mindset Shift, from Smart to Aware, was largely about relationships," she said, pointing to the peak on the right. "Now we are headed over to results."

By the left peak, she drew a squiggly line that resembled a radio wave. "Here we are. We see our competitors with a feature that we don't have, we feel the pain from customers who demand that we have it, we send it over to Ben's team to build, we roll it out, and we feel good again. And then that cycle happens with the next competitor product feature."

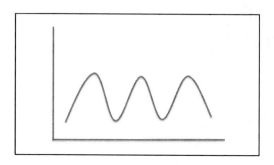

"It's the never-ending problem orientation," Ben agreed.

"It feels good to solve these micro-bursts of issues that come up," said Darryl. "I guess it's not a scalable model, though."

"No, it's not," said Stephanie. "We need to be operating like this, in an outcome orientation." She drew an upward shaping curve. "This is part of the Second Mindset Shift. There are three components to it; we'll tackle the first one today. You know, I struggled with this myself when I led Professional Services. I got stuck focusing solely on the functional area I was leading."

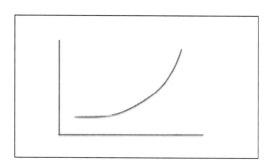

Chapter 9: Cross-Organizational Advocacy

"But Darryl included both me and Peter in the conversation," said Ben. "We're from two very different functional areas, Engineering and Sales."

"That's true, and it's a good start," said Stephanie. "But Darryl's role is a global role, and there weren't key regional leaders at the meeting. We're missing their perspective and the report outs seem to be very US-centric. In addition, you guys keep solving the same problem over and over again. You have to think more systemically about the issue."

Cross-organizational advocacy is the first component of making the shift from a Problem Orientation to an Outcome Orientation.

The first component to making the shift from a *Problem Orientation* to an *Outcome Orientation* is thinking cross-functionally. We call this cross-organizational advocacy, and it's a shift in focus from your own department/ function to a broader view of the organization. Leaders who successfully make this shift begin to ask less of "What is my personal and functional agenda?" and more of "What does the *organization* need?" It's a shift from being very tactically oriented and solving problems in your own functional area, to thinking beyond your function.

To successfully make the shift to an Outcome Orientation, the leader has to appreciate cross-functional collaboration. Further, the leader has to place a higher value on peer relationships than on direct-report relationships.

Here's why:

At the emerging-leader level, the tendency is to solve one problem at a time and usually independently. For example, Engineering managers might be swamped with feature requests that need to be released to the customer, so they ask for more people on their development team. The problem-solving focus is solely on the mindset of the managers taking care of their teams. It's not wrong, it's just not organizationally focused.

An *Outcome Orientation*, on the other hand, requires those same leaders to step back and take a multi-point view about how their resource issues might be related to other areas of the business.

I encourage leaders to expand their thinking about any given problem by considering three perspectives.

1. Self: First, consider your contribution to the issue, challenge, or frustration at hand.

2. External: Second, conduct an external scan of what or who may be contributing to the issue, challenge, or frustration at hand.

3. Systems: Third, consider what system or lack of systems is contributing to the issue, challenge, or frustration at hand.

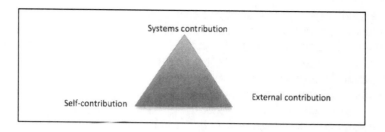

By considering these three perspectives, leaders are forced to address issues outside of their functional area and can thus take a more strategic stance. Perhaps there are constraints that need to be addressed between Engineering and Sales or between Engineering and Product Management.

Here's where things get sticky and why peer relationships become more important than direct-report relationships at the senior leadership level. Solving systemic problems requires leaders to work closely with other areas of the business where they may not have authority. It also places leaders in front of peers who are competing for the same share of resources or even vying for promotion to the same role. It's difficult to be cross-functionally oriented without upsetting your peers if you don't have strong relationships that are built on a foundation of trust and centered on what the organization needs most.

That's precisely why the First Mindset Shift from being *Smart* to *Aware* is so critical, because it enables relationships with those who have competing priorities and career goals.

It's no wonder that senior leaders wish they knew more about relationships, emotional intelligence, and interpersonal agility before being promoted. Their peer relationships depend on that skillset.

10 | Lost and Confused

Ben loved tinkering with technology on the weekends, drawing on his old days as a software engineer. He'd been good at it back in the day, but the more he got promoted, the further it pushed him from the actual technology.

"Take a look at this and let me know what you think," he said, proudly showing Kevin and Jen the prototype he had just built. "I figured it out over the weekend."

"Wow," said Jen.

"Amazing," said Kevin.

"The Product folks are going to be excited," said Ben. "Our customers have been clamoring for this!"

As Ben went off to his 9 a.m. meeting, Kevin and Jen looked at each other.

"He's supposed to be a VP of Engineering, not a software engineer," said Kevin.

"I'm not sure how this is connected to the feature set we already built," said Jen. "It'll take a ton of work to retrofit if this is the direction we want to move in."

Later that afternoon, Ben and Darryl reconvened in Stephanie's office.

"Last time, I mentioned that there were three components to making the Mindset Shift from a Problem Orientation to an Outcome Orientation," said Stephanie, going back to her whiteboard. *"We spoke about the first component of cross-organizational advocacy and the need to think more systemically to move beyond your functional area. Now we're going to discuss the second component, which is about driving a strategic vision. I think this particular topic is timely."*

"Yes, especially given the competition we spoke about last time," said Darryl.

"Ben, I'm glad you uncovered a way to get this feature out," said Stephanie. *"But that's not really the problem here, gentlemen. The problem is that our people are looking for a long-term product direction, not just a quick fix."*

Darryl frowned. *"That sounds fluffy to me,"* he said. *"Ben here created a prototype of the feature our customers are looking for. With just a bit more effort and testing, we could have it released to the market."*

"Darryl, it's a good effort," said Stephanie. *"But frankly, you and Ben aren't working at the right level. Your role as a senior leader is to give up the 'doing' of the work and to create possibilities for the future. It's only with that possibility-based future that people will stick around and follow us into the unknown."*

"We do have to be a source of vision for our people," Ben agreed. *"And I can tell you that the frustration level rises on my team when I rescue others and solve problems that my people should be solving for themselves."*

"The challenge you both have as senior leaders is in balancing near-term priorities with long-term thinking," said Stephanie. *"If you want to be successful operating at the senior-leader level, you have to get more comfortable outside your comfort zone, so to speak. That means broadening not only who you connect with from a cross-organizational advocacy perspective but also broadening both your short- and long-term thinking."*

"But it's so much fun knocking things off my to-do list," Ben joked.

"Yeah," said Darryl. "Sometimes I put things on my to-do list that are already done, just so I can check them off."

Stephanie tried to get them back on track. "There's a certain level of satisfaction and even adrenaline rush that comes from responding to urgent requests and solving immediate problems," she said. "It's not that we will never have these. Of course we will. That's reality. But the shift is to start valuing the time and energy it takes to think longer term, and to show people the possibilities along with the path to getting there. We have to start creating and sharing the BCO-Tek story."

Unite! The 4 Mindset Shifts for Senior Leaders

67

**Driving strategic vision
is the second component
of making the shift from a
Problem Orientation to an
Outcome Orientation.**

Driving strategic vision is about maintaining a broader perspective and longer-term view of the work you do. At the emerging-leader level, the primary focus is usually on what has to be done today or this week. As senior leaders, the focus has to shift to the next six, twelve, eighteen, and even twenty-four months ahead. Without a sound vision, the integration with a newly acquired company or the rollout of a new software development methodology won't mean much to the people you lead.

John Kotter writes in his *Harvard Business Review* article on "Leading Change" that when they studied failed transformation efforts, they often found plans, directives, and programs in place, but rarely was there a clear and compelling vision. The mind-numbing details were there, but team members rarely understood the direction, what was it in for them, or why the changes were being made. The result? People felt alienated and confused.

It doesn't have to be this way. Even if you don't consider yourself "visionary," respond to the following three questions that Andrew Neitlick asks in his book, *Elegant Leadership*:

Are you a source of vision? In other words, are you showing up in this world painting the picture of the future, or are you complaining about the logistical inconveniences that we often find in major change efforts? Is the future exciting? Is it a picture that others want to be a part of? You can be a source of vision in all aspects of your work—for your team or organization, for the quality of service you provide, for your career, for your team members' careers, for the culture of the organization, and even for the three-week project that just landed on your desk.

Are you a source of possibilities? It's hard to inspire people with a vision if the future isn't positive. Your positivity doesn't have to be inauthentic. It can be real, vulnerable, and positive at the same time—inspiring *realistic* hope. Being a source of possibilities means having conversations about how things can be. It means looking beyond the complaints, constraints, and criticism and remaining open long enough to imagine a different outcome or possibility.

Are you a source for finding greater meaning in your work? Leaders who begin to develop their capacity to focus more on the future also find more significant personal meaning in their work. Their work becomes less about processing benefits or selling software or building widgets. It becomes about making a meaningful contribution to our work and our world.

Make Time for Vision

How much time do you need in your role to focus on the future and drive a vision? It might not be as much as you think: 10 percent? 20 percent? 30 percent? For the sake of argument, let's say that 20 percent of your time should be focused on vision. That's only eight hours a week, assuming a 40-hour workweek. (I know, you probably work closer to 50 or more hours a week!)

If you don't schedule time to work on your vision, you'll likely never get around to it. There will always be something more urgent. But if you break down eight hours a week over five days, that's just a little over 1.6 hours a day. Schedule it and it will get done.

Also, schedule it at a time when you are most focused and have the greatest mental capacity. For me, that's early in the morning. I know that if I try to schedule strategic thinking or writing late in the afternoon, I have a very low likelihood of getting it done. Figure out what time works best for you, and schedule it.

11 Build People Capacity

"Wait, Ben, this is important," Peter said as the leadership team meeting broke up. Michael and Adriana had already left, and Stephanie was busy packing up her materials.

"I know. I just have to get back to 'real work,'" said Ben, making air quotes on that last remark.

The hiring issue had come up again. Two more engineers had left the organization in search of newer and more exciting opportunities. Apparently, they just didn't "see the vision," according to their exit interviews.

"We also need to teach our people better skills on how to fire people," said Ben. "We're tolerating way too much. The bottom line is that we have some underperformers who have managed to stick around while this company shifted from founder-led to a more mature and focused organization, and now we need a different skillset to scale the business."

"Sorry to interrupt, gentlemen," said Stephanie, overhearing them. "Ben, to some extent, you're right. As the company grows, our people need to grow, and we as leaders need to develop new skillsets too. But the issue isn't that your people need to learn how to fire employees. Your team is

ultimately a reflection of you as the leader, and the need to fire people is symptomatic of other issues."

"What kind of issues?" asked Darryl, jumping in.

"The root cause could be in your hiring process, for example," Stephanie explained. "Or with how you are onboarding and developing your people."

Ben pursed his lips. Stephanie's understated comment about people being a reflection of the leader hit him hard. "That's the third component, isn't it?" he said. "The third part of making a shift to an outcome orientation."

Stephanie smiled. "You have to see people development as 'real work,'" she said, mimicking Ben's air quotes. "At your level, people are the real work."

They agreed to reconvene to discuss the issue further. The departing engineers obviously had to be replaced, and there were performance issues on both Ben and Darryl's teams. On top of that, there were growing hiring needs in Sales.

Ben was anxious about this hiring situation, but he was also ready for the weekend so that he could disconnect from work. He had another mountain rescue practice coming up. He was working hard to get to the next leadership level there, and it required both a deep understanding of technical rescue systems and a solid demonstration of his ability to lead rescuers in the field. It wasn't uncommon for Ben to spend his entire Saturday working through different rescue scenarios with more senior members of the team.

The scenario for this weekend started with a "page" from the 911 system: "Injured hiker on Mount Sanitas." That was a common place for hikers both new and experienced, and there were several hiking trails where the incident could happen.

On Saturday, Ben arrived at the scene and began devising a plan. He called in one of the more experienced team members. He calmly assigned another team member to start gathering gear they might need. Typical of many rescue missions, they began with a search, as the 911 information about the patient location was not always accurate. The first step in that process was to assess the terrain, create search teams, and find the patient. Ben also had to think ahead about when and where to position gear to make the evacuation as efficient as possible.

Ninety minutes later, after the scenario and the debrief, Ben sat on a rock near the trailhead with the team leader, who was also a friend. "What feedback do you have for me, John, based on the mission today?" Ben asked.

John pulled out a small compression sack that had a mix of chocolate, peanuts, and pretzels, and offered some to Ben. "On the plus side," John started, "excellent progress since your last time as Site Lead. You remained calm and you delegated well."

Ben nodded and took a swig from his water bottle.

"Now, areas for improvement," said John. "You're still getting stuck in a few tasks that others should be doing. I noticed you managing the rope during the first pitch of the evacuation. That pulls you away from thinking longer term about what the team needs on the next pitch. For example, you had to send someone back to the truck to get another bash kit with the extra belay device; on a real mission, that could have set us back 30 minutes in getting the patient out of the field."

Ben asked a few clarifying questions before they began to wrap up. "I appreciate the feedback," said Ben. "I also appreciate you spending the entire day with me. After all, today isn't an official practice."

"Nothing's more important, Ben," John replied. "Our future depends on having well-trained technical rescuers who can also lead others in the field. As the group leader, my responsibility now has shifted from doing the rescues to making sure we have others who can do them. It's difficult, because you know that I love being in the field, but that's ultimately my role now."

Ben nodded. "That's the real work," he said.

The third component of an Outcome Orientation: building people capacity.

Building people capacity is truly about investment throughout a team member's employment life cycle—from hiring to development to succession. The real shift for leaders is seeing the work it takes to interview, hire, coach, and develop people as "real work."

Think about the time commitment it takes to hire a new employee, or the dedication needed to mentor and coach up-and-comers. How about the tireless hours of assessing and preparing high potentials for promotion? There always seem to be more urgent items competing for a leader's attention, which is why most senior leaders fail in making the shift from a *Problem Orientation* to an *Outcome Orientation*.

Building people capacity is never about the urgent. It's always about the important. This shift is ultimately about embracing your role as a multiplier across the people you lead. In other words, you can put an hour into task-related work and you'll get an hour of output in return, or you can put an hour into onboarding and developing others and you'll get a multiple of that in output as you enable others going forward.

Building people capacity starts with selection. Jim Collins in his best-selling book, *Good to Great*, talks about three simple truths when it comes to selecting the right leaders:

- Begin with "who" rather than "what." When you have the right people on your team, it doesn't matter what your strategy is, because they will likely adapt.

- When you have the right people, you spend less time managing and motivating them. The right people don't need to be tightly managed and motivated because they're self-motivated. That enables you and every leader beneath you to operate at the right level.

- If you have the wrong people on your team, it doesn't matter if you discover the right direction. You still won't have a great company.

In addition to the "Three Truths" above, leaders have to hire people who are coachable. Without coachability, even a team member with the critical technical and industry knowledge will never achieve total potential. When senior leaders truly value the selection process and create a culture where others do too, everything downstream in a team member's employment life cycle is easier.

Building people capacity next involves development. Senior leaders have to spend time developing the managers and team members beneath them. It's absolutely critical to the long-term success and scalability of the business. But the leader has to see "coaching" as valuable work. That means creating clear expectations and communicating a consistent vision. It means being visible and providing feedback and recognition when coachable moments appear. It also means conducting regular one-on-one coaching sessions that are less transactional (e.g., task and project management oriented) and more developmental.

Finally, building people capacity scales upward with succession planning. Great senior leaders are constantly assessing their leadership bench to ensure people are prepared for their next role. They identify high-potential leaders and provide them with the coaching, challenging projects, and career planning they need to succeed in the future. They also identify team members who are in the wrong roles and quickly find a better fit or elegantly move them out of the organization.

For the self-aware leader, shifting from a *Problem Orientation* to an *Outcome Orientation* can be learned relatively quickly. It can have a powerful multiplier impact on the organization.

Reflection Questions – Mindset Shift 2: From a Problem Orientation to an Outcome Orientation

Reflect on the following questions to help you make the shift from a *Problem Orientation* to an *Outcome Orientation*:

- Are you involving the right people and departments to solve systemic problems?
- Are you thinking beyond your own team and department?
- Do you consider what other functional areas would say or ask when making a decision?
- How much time do you allocate on your calendar for strategic thinking?
- Are you a source of possibilities?
- Are you a source of vision?

- Are you a source for helping others find greater meaning in their work?

- What are you doing to improve the hiring and interviewing practices in your organization?

- Are you developing your people to be better at interviewing and assessing people?

- How much time do you spend coaching the managers who work for you?

- Do you have a succession plan for yourself and others on your team?

Mindset Shift 3

Unite! The 4 Mindset Shifts for Senior Leaders

79

12 Mindset Shift 3 – From Getting Compliance and Consensus to Winning Commitment

Ben, Jen, Kevin, and two other software engineers sat in their weekly meeting, reviewing the status of backlog issues in planning for the upcoming development sprint.

"I thought we fixed that issue," said Ben. "I gave you a solution two weeks ago."

Jen and Kevin looked at each other. "We appreciated you reaching out with a suggestion," said Jen, "but the idea didn't really integrate well with the plans we already had for this last sprint of development."

"But the fix worked," Ben protested. "I've seen similar solutions on other development teams."

Jen and Kevin responded concisely, as they had learned to do with Ben's dominant personality style. They outlined the key steps they thought would deliver a good solution. As they spoke, Ben crossed his arms and began jiggling his right foot. He countered as soon as they had finished.

"The solution I came up with will have a more immediate impact on our product," he said. Then he went on with more details for a full two minutes.

Jen tried to jump in with an additional suggestion, but Ben always led the discussion back to the solution he was advocating.

Kevin and Jen finally caved. They knew from experience that there was no moving Ben once he had made up his mind.

"I wish he would at least acknowledge our ideas," Jen said after the meeting was over and Ben had left the room. "We are experienced senior technology managers. We have a perspective."

Over on the Product team, Darryl was also wrestling with some critical challenges. "It's one of those weeks, isn't it, folks?" he said as he wrapped up the weekly meeting.

On the surface, the environment was collegial and harmonious. Darryl had rambled on for about five minutes and then asked, "Any questions?" A few heads nodded, one team member looked at his watch, and another looked up from her phone. Of the five people in the room, no one responded.

"Great, sounds like we have consensus," said Darryl. "Let's check our progress in next week's meeting."

As the last two team members walked out together, one asked, "Do you think this is the right approach?"

"No, I don't," said the other. "I have no idea what the plan is."

Getting compliance and consensus is not the same as winning commitment.

Unite! The 4 Mindset Shifts for Senior Leaders

83

The Shift

Our work with senior leaders, both through coaching and confidential verbal interviews, has revealed that one of the biggest complaints team members report about their senior leaders is a lack of transparent communication. Of course, when you ask senior leaders, they often think they are over-communicating.

The result of this perception of the lack of transparent communication is a reduced level of trust and feeling valuable. In turn, there is an impact on the business: slower decision-making, and misalignment due to a lack of commitment.

This leads us to our third Mindset Shift in our Unite! Leadership Model that senior leaders need to make, which is a shift from *Focusing on Compliance or Consensus to Winning Commitment.*

Imagine a continuum that describes two polar opposite communication styles. On one end, let's say the left side, is an aggressive style. The opposite end, to the right, is a passive style. This third shift to successfully transitioning into a senior leadership role requires a shift to the middle of the continuum, depending on whether your leadership style tends to be more on the aggressive end of communication or its opposite, the passive end. The result will be an organization full of people who are committed to what they are doing, and not merely complying or conceding because they feel they must or have given up.

The Passive Side

If your tendencies are more like Darryl's, on the passive side, the shift is moving from a focus on getting consensus to a focus on winning commitment. If your tendencies tend to be more like Ben's, on the aggressive side of the continuum, the shift is to move from a focus on getting compliance to a focus on winning commitment.

On the passive side of the equation, the tendency is to be a people pleaser, where the leader is overly concerned about making everyone happy and gaining agreement from all the stakeholders. There's an avoidance tendency that comes with this style as the leader tolerates behaviors that are unacceptable in the workplace.

Take, for example, the president of a fast-growing technology company we worked with recently. His head of Finance is an extremely competent technician who knows funding and the world of IPOs as well as anyone. The challenge was that at times, the head of Finance's behavior was considered "abusive." The president was aware of this. He had experienced it in team meetings and hadn't addressed it, at least not to anyone's knowledge. His main concern was to make everyone happy—the head of Finance, the investors, and the leadership team. For this leader, maintaining stability and a supportive environment was a priority, but the challenge was that his passivity was making him overly tolerant of unprofessional and even egregious outbreaks. He, too, had to learn how to move his communication style more to the middle of the spectrum, away from over-passivity.

The consequential decisions at the senior leadership level are too complicated to focus on agreement and making everyone happy. They involve too many constituents and stakeholders. So, the shift for the more passive leader is from focusing on getting consensus to winning commitment.

There is a distinction between consensus and commitment. In consensus, we focus on getting everyone to a point where they agree to move forward. The process is slow and more suited to bowling outings and company picnic decisions. Commitment, on the other hand, requires a courageous leader to run toward and not away from dialogue, debate, and conflict, encouraging everyone to get their ideas out on the table. Not with the goal of seeking consensus, but to ensure that everyone's voice is truly heard. When people feel genuinely and authentically heard, they are likely to buy into a decision that is made—even if they disagree with that decision.

The Aggressive Side

Going back to our communications continuum, an aggressive leader like Ben, with his laser-focused results orientation, tends to formulate his vision and immediately implement it. Leaders like this are usually motivated by change, challenge, and controlling their environment and don't spend much time getting anyone's buy-in. Or, they recognize that they need buy-in and ask for input simply to garner support for their position, not because they care what others have to say. As a result, people tend to be compliant around this pushy style instead of owning and being committed to the direction in which the organization will move. It's not uncommon for team members to spend an enormous amount of time managing around these leaders who are set in their way of doing things and demonstrate an unwillingness to bend. Such leaders come across as trying to convince others as to why their idea is best, versus actually listening and embracing alternate ideas. They are often distanced from the truth of what goes on in an organization. People respond by either complying, or they ignore the input and do their own thing anyway. Either way, reactions are driven by the leader's unapproachable style and fear of repercussion.

The consequential decisions at the senior-leader level are too important for simply gaining compliance from people. In the end, decisions will get revisited over and over, and the priorities that are most important to the leader—action and results—will ultimately take longer. So the shift for the more aggressive leader is from focusing on getting compliance to winning commitment.

The Result

Making this shift to focusing on winning commitment, instead of on getting consensus or on compliance, is ultimately about winning the hearts and minds of people. This is about building the commitment you see from employees at companies like Trader Joe's, Apple, Patagonia, Google, and Method. At the emerging-leader level, it was easier, as most leaders were focused only on their work team and only a few people had to deal with their dreaded dysfunction. At the senior-leadership level, there is a higher level of complexity, as leaders often have to influence others over whom they have no authority.

13 Building Commitment through Intentional Conversation

At a morning meeting with Product, Engineering, and Sales, the team was beginning to see the need for organizational change.

"It's clear to me that we have to create better alignment," said Peter. "Having the marketing team separated out from Sales is creating unnecessary communication breakdowns between how we initially attract customers and then sell to them. I think we need to move marketing back under my group."

"I've got great relationships with the marketing folks," said Darryl. "I'm not sure how they'll respond, but I agree that moving the marketing folks from my team to Peter's will give me more time to focus on Product Strategy, which is really where I should be positioned to best support future growth."

Stephanie was delighted to see that her team members were all coming to the same conclusion. Everyone knew it would create more alignment. It hadn't been about ego; it had just taken time for everyone to realize that the current organizational structure was slowing the ability to respond to fast-changing market needs.

"All right, I'm meeting with my Engineering managers this afternoon and I'll let them know," said Ben.

"I can also connect with my Sales Team today," said Peter. "I'm sure they'll be good with it."

Darryl piped up, "Uh, guys. No offense, but the marketing folks like working for me. This is going to be a major change for them."

"Listen, they can either get on the train or let it pass by," said Ben. "We have to move quickly in this competitive space."

Stephanie let the conversation continue, hoping there would be some disagreement, but Darryl finally gave in to Ben and Peter's strong opinions to move quickly. She went back over to her whiteboard to the Mount Results and Mount Relationships map.

"Peter," said Stephanie. "Ben and Darryl have been brainstorming the last few weeks about what it takes to successfully make the transition into senior leadership. This is a model that was passed down to me when I was running Professional Services."

"You mean you didn't just make this up on the fly?" Darryl joked.

"We talked about the first Mindset Shift—from being smart to being aware," Stephanie continued. "That's on the relationship side of the equation. Leaders have to understand their impact on others if they want to forge strong relationships with other senior leaders who will often have competing priorities."

Stephanie then pointed to the left side of the model. "We also talked about the second Mindset Shift—shifting from a problem orientation to an outcome orientation. The keys to making this shift were to (1) embrace the need for cross-functional advocacy, (2) communicate the vision and possibilities for the future, and (3) recognize that building people capacity is your 'real work' as a senior leader."

"No wonder we've been working better together, Ben," said Peter. "You've been getting great coaching. How do I get in on this?"

"You're in on it now, Peter," said Stephanie. "The third shift is kind of a dual shift. It involves moving from either getting consensus to winning commitment, or from getting compliance to winning commitment, based on your particular communication style."

"Let me guess," said Darryl. "Today we're back on Mount Relationships."

"Correct," said Stephanie.

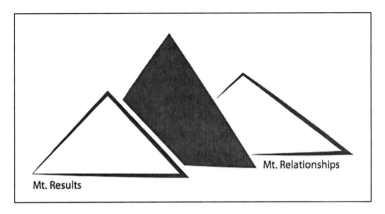

"Ben, pay close attention," said Darryl. Ben shot him a smirk.

"The organizational change we are proposing today is significant," said Stephanie. "It's not as if we're just moving people to different parts of the office. Reporting lines will change, workflows will change, and your team members will have to get comfortable with new leaders. While this change won't result in jobs lost or anything that severe, it will certainly be a disruption, and many people will feel a loss. To Darryl's point, we need to be more intentional in the way we communicate this change."

"How do we do that?" asked Peter.

"For one, we have to overcome the individual tendencies that come with our preferences toward either results or relationships. For example, Ben, we've talked about how your aggressive tendencies often result in compliance from others. Darryl, your tendency toward being overly agreeable often leads to an aura of consensus."

"Yeah, but we're both getting things done," Ben pointed out. "We're both good producers."

"Absolutely," Stephanie agreed. "That's why you're in senior-leader roles. But to be successful at this level, you have to move away from compliance, Ben. And you, Darryl, have to move away from consensus. This next shift is a shift toward winning real commitment."

Tool #1:
Use intentional communication to make the Shift to Building Commitment.

How do you make the Mindset Shift from focusing on getting consensus or compliance to winning real commitment? I believe there are three critical components that leaders need to embrace to win the hearts of their people. The first is to create structured and intentional communication.

This piece of the commitment puzzle is about being intentional with your messaging and using all available channels of communication in a systematic way. It's about ensuring that you and other leaders on your leadership team are communicating the same or similar message that is aligned with the company direction. It's also about using multiple communication channels to spread your message consistently every day. John Kotter, in his classic *Harvard Business Review* article, "Leading Change," talks about the power of ten leaders sending ten messages every day instead of solely relying on the all-hands meeting as the primary channel of communication.

Here are some critical considerations when creating structured communication:

- Who is the target audience?
- What do you want your audience to do or think differently as a result of your communication with them?
- How do you want them to feel?
- What are the three key messages that need to get cascaded?
- What vehicles/communication channels can you use on a daily basis?
- What is the frequency and cadence of that communication?

Structured communication tends to be more challenging for leaders who are spontaneous in nature and do things on the fly. It may also take more energy for the introverted leader with the natural tendency to do things from behind a computer. Creating and delivering structured communication requires getting out in front and connecting with people—intentionally—at every turn, from the chance encounter around the proverbial water cooler to your regular team meeting.

14 Communicating the Big Why

Ben, Darryl, Peter, and Stephanie had stayed focused on how they would build commitment to the structural change of moving marketing from Darryl's organization over to Sales.

"Okay, I can communicate those messages with my team this afternoon," Ben said as he began to pack his laptop and notes. He looked around to see that no one else was standing up.

"Here we go again," said Darryl.

The conversation wasn't quite over.

"Ben, what's most important to you?" asked Stephanie.

"Getting stuff done," said Ben. "Results."

"And what happens when your people haven't bought in to a common direction?"

Ben sighed. "Yes, I see where you're going with that," he said. "It takes me longer to get the results I want most."

"Exactly," said Stephanie. "Intentional and structured communication is important, but there are two more parts to building commitment. The second component is communicating what I call The Big Why. People want to know the rationale behind

a decision or a change in direction. Tell them why something needs to get done and they'll be much more likely to be committed to doing it."

"Good point," said Peter. He gave Ben a significant look. "The last time someone told me to do something without explaining the rationale, I got the job done, but I also unconsciously undermined the effort by complaining to co-workers."

"When that happens, I tend to get defensive," added Ben.

"You, defensive?" said Darryl. "Nah."

"Oh, you're on fire today, buddy," said Ben.

Tool #2:
People need to understand the "Big Why."

When I was going through Ranger School as a young Army officer and the instructor told us to head out on a fifteen-mile road march, we just did it. No questions asked. That might sound like blind obedience, but it wasn't. We knew exactly why the Ranger instructors put us through hell. They wanted to weed out people who weren't cut out to be Rangers.

When commanders create their mission orders, they always include a statement called "commander's intent." The idea was that you always know why you were being sent out on a mission. It frees you up to make decisions when there isn't clarity.

In my normal day-to-day world, as I'm traveling to client sites and sitting on a plane wondering why the flight is delayed, I'm less likely to have empathy for the situation when I don't know why I am sitting on the tarmac and not moving. When the pilot announces that we can't leave because of weather or a mechanical situation, I might not be happy, but at least I understand why. I don't have to put any energy into resenting a situation I don't understand. A simple text alert from my favorite airline letting me know that my flight is delayed sucks, but it's better than arriving at the airport sixty minutes early for no reason.

Instead of making a change and then just expecting others to accept it and comply, offer the following:

- Discuss the alternatives that were considered.
- Tell people what you know and what you don't know—and why.
- Acknowledge how the decision will affect everyone.

At the end of the day, your team members appreciate transparency and openness, even if the decision may negatively affect them. Transparency and openness also make people feel like they are trusted, respected, and connected to their organization—instead of being left in the dark. And when people understand why, it helps establishes a sense of urgency for next steps.

15 Allow for Dialogue

Stephanie had explained that the first part of moving from getting consensus or compliance to winning commitment was intentional messaging. The second was explaining the Big Why. Ben, Darryl, and Peter were now entering the home stretch of how to build commitment around the organizational change of moving marketing back under Peter's responsibility.

"The third part is about allowing room for dialogue," said Stephanie.

"That makes sense," said Peter. "I know that in Sales, our customers never respond favorably when we just tell them something. Most of the time we engage with them so we can understand their perspective and work to uncover what's most important to them."

"That's exactly right," said Stephanie. "The first two steps, intentional communication and explaining the Big Why, are structured and almost one-way. They help ensure we are sending an aligned message as senior leaders. But the true part of engagement/commitment only comes when other people are involved in the conversation."

"People want to feel valued," said Darryl.

"Without a doubt," agreed Stephanie. "If I could only impart one leadership lesson that I've learned *in my career, that would be it. People want to feel like they are valued. Without that, they won't be committed."*

"What if they disagree with the decision we've made?" asked Darryl.

"Good question," said Stephanie. "Chances are good that we'll make important and consequential decisions for this business that aren't always popular. Our roles as leaders is not to make decisions based on whether people like us, but whether they add value to the business, employees, and shareholders as a whole."

Peter jumped in. "If people feel valued and that they've been heard, they're more likely to get onboard," he said.

"True," said Stephanie. "Remember, we aren't seeking agreement. We're seeking commitment. And commitment only comes when people know that their leaders have truly heard their perspective."

Ben shifted in his chair. "I have to admit," he said, "my tendency is to move pretty quickly and not allow for much dialogue."

"And how's that working for you?" asked Stephanie with a wry smile.

"Well, sometimes I propose technical solutions and they don't get implemented," said Ben, giving Darryl a look. "We end up revisiting those decisions over and over. Seriously, though, I can see now that without involving anyone in the discussion, my team members remain uncommitted to the decisions that I thought we just made."

"And then we get meeting after meeting," agreed Peter.

"The same thing happens to me, but for different reasons," said Darryl. "I don't truly engage my team. I ask them if they have questions, but if they just nod their heads or say yes, I let it go at that. Then we wind up talking about the same issues next time, even when I thought those issues were resolved."

"It's not rocket science," said Stephanie. "But it does take time. And this is the 'real work' of being a senior leader. We could come up with the best technology or the best process or the best idea, but if we can't build commitment with our people, it won't matter."

Tool #3:
Make space for dialogue.

Unite! The 4 Mindset Shifts for Senior Leaders

99

Creating structured communication and explaining the "Big Why" are about making communication intentional. Both components are important yet not sufficient—largely because they have a one-way focus. The third and perhaps most important component of building commitment is allowing for dialogue.

Genuine and pure dialogue gives people the freedom and opportunity to let you know the truth. This two-way conversation is where true interaction occurs, as leaders engage people not just in formal settings, such as the all-hands meeting, but also at every opportunity, from the chance encounter to the scheduled team meeting.

In a staff meeting, for example, you might let people know ahead of time that you are looking for their input so that they come prepared. You may also mine for conflict, as Patrick Lencioni describes in *The Five Dysfunctions of a Team*, where you literally go around the room and ask each person for their perspective. You can utilize your 1-1 coaching sessions with a "check-in" at the beginning of each conversation, generating a less transactional and more developmental discussion. Or, you might notice someone in the hallway and take half a minute to address the issue.

This is an opportunity to create a communication plan that uses multiple channels to engage people in the business and ultimately move them to a place where they know and feel they've been heard.

We've noticed in our leadership development work that people often go through three distinct levels as they mature as leaders when it comes to dialogue and engaging with people.

- At Level 1, leaders consider themselves the expert and want to be seen as smart, strong, and knowledgeable. As a result, they generally don't ask people for their input, but set directives. This is the classic infallible leader.

- At Level 2, leaders realize that they need to get others on board with their particular vision. To that end, they ask for their input but mostly to appease others and gain buy-in.

- At Level 3, a more mature level that most leaders never reach, leaders ask for other people's ideas. Why? Because they actually want to hear and consider them. Allowing for dialogue enables you to win the hearts and minds of your people. This is the ultimate commitment, where people go above and beyond, and they mostly do it because they know they were heard and thus feel valued.

Case Study

Jim is the president of a $600-million manufacturing business. His leadership team of eleven spent over six months developing the company's five-year strategy. The market research, competitive analysis, dialogue, and debate set the context for the plan—the "Big Why." When this results-oriented leadership team rolled out the plan to more than 500 employees, they focused on sharing the content—the objectives, work plans, information, and details. That makes sense, right? They're a data-driven organization, and the employees got all the data.

But people rarely make change based on data alone. They need to feel emotionally connected to decisions. Fortunately for this team, they recognized that their over-emphasis on results was coming before their focus on sharing the why and engaging their people in dialogue about the company's future. They were able to pivot in time and save their efforts.

This is an all-too-common scenario for the typical results-oriented senior leadership team. The dialogue internally has already happened. The plans are formulated. Now they are ready to execute. The problem is that no one else in the organization has had a chance to do the same processing that the leadership team did, and they aren't yet ready to be on board.

As senior leaders, you have to provide both content and context. One without the other rarely leads to true commitment. Content is simply the information about the topic at hand: the data, the project plans, and the next steps. The context, however, is everything we've talked about here: the structured messaging, the rationale behind the decision, and the dialogue with people so they are filled with the information you want them to have instead of the stories they've made up themselves.

16 Rescue Practice

That weekend, Ben met John for another round of extra practice. They started pulling gear from the rescue truck, a converted Ford F250 that was highly organized and could store enough rescue equipment for several missions simultaneously.

Ben looked at the litter, the metal basket shaped like a backboard that could hold a patient during mountain rescue missions. "It's taking us forever to get the new litter in service," he said as he unloaded it from the truck. "When are we going to make a decision on this?"

John responded patiently as he took one end of the litter and helped Ben place it on the ground. "This is a major change in our rescue system," said John. "We have to take time to ensure people know why we're using it, know how to use it properly, and do the testing on it in the real field environment."

"You sound like my boss at work," said Ben with a laugh. "We're going through a minor reorganization that's going to shift a few jobs around, and she's been talking about intentional messages, explaining why we're making the change and allowing others time to engage in dialogue around it."

"That's partly why it seemingly takes so long," said John. "People need time to experience the new rescue system, ask questions, and understand how the change is going to affect them. Heck, they'll likely have some pretty good process-improvement ideas we haven't thought of."

Reflection Questions – Mindset Shift 3: From Focusing on Getting Compliance and Consensus to Winning Commitment.

Unite! The 4 Mindset Shifts for Senior Leaders

105

Reflect on the following questions to help you make this third Mindset Shift from getting compliance or getting consensus to winning commitment:

- What business changes are you currently in the process of making or know you will be making soon?
- What are the top three critical messages that people need to hear?
- What communication channels can you leverage to send your messages?
- What is the rationale behind your decisions?
- What do you hope will be achieved as a result of the decision?
- How can you allow for dialogue to occur?
- How open are you to actually listening to what people may say or suggest?

Mindset Shift 4

17 Mindset Shift 4 – From Task Manager to Evangelist

As Darryl was heading over to Ben's office, he bumped into a group of Jen and Kevin's software engineers and designers hanging out in one of the collaboration areas. It was a comfortable setting with bright orange couches in a U-shape around a 60-inch TV. Employees at BCO-Tek used the space to huddle and brainstorm about issues and opportunities.

As Darryl walked by, he stopped and said, "Hey, folks. What are you working on?"

"We're strategizing on some UI changes for the next sprint." The UI, otherwise known as the user interface, was constantly being assessed to help make the customer experience better.

"Nice," said Darryl, peering to get a better look at the TV screen projecting some of their latest ideas. "Have you seen what our competitors are doing with the accounts landing page?"

After a few nods, he went on for a few minutes about the benefits of some of the latest design techniques. He concluded with, "Looking forward to seeing what you create. Send it over when you have a demo."

The group was beaming. It sure felt good to get feedback from a senior leader in the organization.

A day later, after leaving one of their team meetings, Kevin and Jen were livid. Whatever happened with Darryl's interaction the day before had sent their team members on a wild ride. They were proud of the changes they presented, but soon they realized that those changes were out of alignment with Kevin and Jen's expectations. The vision that was laid out for the quarter had been thrown out of whack by Darryl's helicopter interaction, like a protective parent swooping in to save the day.

Kevin threw up his hands. "If Darryl wants to manage the project, fine. Let him. I've got plenty of other things to focus on."

"He is a vice president, isn't he?" asked Jen.

"Sometimes I wonder."

Mindset Shift #4: From Task Manager to Evangelist.

Unite! The 4 Mindset Shifts for Senior Leaders

111

When we asked *executive* leaders to describe what effective *senior* leaders do, their responses overwhelmingly centered on empowering people and building others up. They said that their successful senior leaders were able to stay involved at the right level without micromanaging. They had high standards, operated at the right level, and held their people accountable.

That brings us to the fourth Mindset Shift in our Unite! Leadership Model that senior leaders need to make to be successful: from *Task Manager* to *Evangelist*.

There is a big distinction between a Task Manager and being an Evangelist for something. Managing tasks is important and critical work at every level within an organization, but as a guiding orientation, it's narrow, siloed, and mostly about getting things done. Being an Evangelist, on the other hand, is about being a supporter or representative or leader of a cause. While the Task Manager is focused on maintaining status quo and efficiency, the Evangelist is focused on ensuring that the right things are being done in alignment with the vision and guiding direction of the organization.

We recently consulted for a fast-growing high-tech company. The organization had grown from the typical start-up to a $150-million company with almost 200 employees. Growth projections looked good, and the company expected to add personnel over the coming years. Most of the leadership team had been with the company from its founding, and two leaders maintained primary ownership.

Even with all this growth, the CTO had yet to make the shift to Evangelist. He was the quintessential tech guru who loved to code. He spent his weekends building applications for fun, and during the week, he loved to dive into the weeds. At an early stage of a start-up, that's exactly what leaders need to do. But to scale a business and create a sustainable organization, he was operating at the wrong level by failing to provide a strategic technology direction for the organization and champion that direction through execution. He was the classic executive operating as a project manager.

The bottom line is that Evangelists drive execution to bring the organizational vision into reality, but they do it strategically.

Strategic versus Task

At the emerging-leader level, leaders have to learn how to reallocate their time to complete their work and also help align the work of others. As senior leaders, they have to step up and learn to balance the urgency of the day-to-day with important, longer-term initiatives of the area they lead. It's the classic balance of urgent versus important, but at a functional level within the organization. *The E-Myth*, by Michael Gerber, describes it as "double vision," seeing and making decisions based on two realities. The first reality is your current situation: employees, customers, and commitments. The second reality is the future: your dream, your vision, and how the organization will be when this vision is realized.

The crux of this Mindset Shift is being able to go from "doing" the work to getting the work done through others while maintaining an eye on the future. To make this shift, leaders have to see leadership itself as "real work." They have to embrace the time it takes to craft and communicate vision, hire winning talent, develop people, and be committed to leadership-team meetings. You'll know you've made the shift when you see these types of focus areas as "want-to-do work" versus "need-to-do work."

Task versus Strategic Shifts

Task Focus	Strategic Focus
Making decisions based on functional needs first.	Making decisions based on business needs first.
Competing for resources based on functional needs first.	Competing for resources based on business needs first.
Collaboration occurs mostly in functional areas, creating silos across the organization.	Thinking shifts to a systems perspective, where the leader has the agility to take other functional areas into account.
Operational and day-to-day orientation first.	Strategic orientation drives day-to-day priorities.
Time is mostly spent focused on urgent items.	A leader's calendar has time blocked off for strategic thinking and people development.
Leadership-team meetings take the leader away from "real work."	Leadership-team meetings are valued and an important part of the leader's role.
Individual ego and agenda first.	Relentless drive and passion for the organization first.

18 It's All a Priority

"Man, I'm swamped," said Jen. She and Kevin had just left an all-hands meeting where the head of People Operations announced a move to a new compensation and talent-management process. "With all these meetings, I can't seem to find the time to get any real work done."

"Yeah, I've been working late nights after the kids go down," said Kevin. "It's the only time I can get things done without interruption."

Back at their desks, Jen quickly signed onto her laptop and scrolled through her email, looking for the messages that seemed most important. A message from Ben, with the subject line "Action Requested," stood out. Uh-oh, it's the business continuity project, she thought. She hadn't had time to focus at all on getting the server information over to the IT team

From the sound of Ben's email, he seemed frustrated. Jen shot off a quick response to let him know she'd get the information to IT within the hour.

A moment later, she responded to an email from People Operations about the rollout plan for the new compensation system. She switched over to a message from Darryl about a question on developing a high-priority product feature change for a customer and also creating a report that marketing needed to better understand conversation rates. Already a few minutes late for her next meeting, she ran into one of her software engineers who had been waiting over a day for her approval on their go-forward plan for the next development sprint.

It wasn't much different for Kevin. He'd been tasked with implementing a new software-code management system from Engineering and providing input on a new interviewing class that People Operations was developing.

Ben was also feeling the stress when he walked into Stephanie's office. Peter and Darryl were chatting about the upcoming Denver Broncos game; it was shaping up to be another winning season.

Stephanie got them started. "I began this discussion with each of you earlier this week in our quick quarterly reviews about the final switchback over to the results side of the equation," she said, pointing to Mount Results and Relationships on her whiteboard. "From Task Manager to Evangelist."

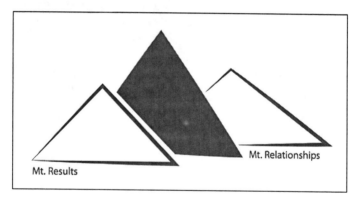

"I think I'm speaking for Ben, too, when I say our tendency is overly hands-on with tasks," said Peter.

"I'm pretty hands-on too," Darryl piped up. "I just tend to do it from behind the safety of my computer." He got a chuckle.

"One of my observations is that employees at BCO-Tek are generally struggling with understanding our top priorities," said Stephanie. "Part of being an Evangelist is helping them understand what's most important to the business."

"We're definitely struggling with that in Engineering," said Ben. "Just a few minutes ago, I got an email from Jen saying that she prioritized some of her other tasks over the business continuity project we have going on right now."

"Okay," said Stephanie. "In the absence of clarity of what's most important to the business, our people will make decisions that aren't in alignment with our organizational priorities. As an Evangelist, we have to preach every day about those priorities to ensure that people are working on the right things."

"Yeah, and the challenge is to ensure that we let go of most of the task work at this level," added Darryl. "That's the primary challenge I have right now."

"This Mindset Shift is largely about seeing leadership as real work," Stephanie reminded them. "It's not something you just layer on top of the technical function that you lead."

She had them open their laptops. "Let's do a calendar test," she said.

"Huh?" said Darryl.

"We can tell pretty quickly if you're operating at the right level simply by the choices you are making about what's on your calendar," Stephanie explained. "Let's see if any of those choices reflect how you are setting the right priorities with your team."

Both Ben and Darryl gulped.

Evangelists create focus.

One of the first symptoms we see with senior leaders who struggle to be Evangelists is with their direct reports. It's classic overwhelm: too many priorities. There are twelve goals for the quarter or twenty-two priorities for the year, and guess what? They're all number-one priorities.

We recently worked with a leadership team from a national retail office-supply company. It quickly became clear why the team was struggling with understanding their priorities when we saw the strategic plan for their division: a menu of twenty-one different items. How do you choose where to start? When everything is the top priority, nothing is a priority. People lack clarity on what's most important to their organization, because everything is important.

Merriam-Webster defines "priority" as something more important than other things and that needs to be done or dealt with first. Making the transition from Task Manager to Evangelist puts senior leaders in a role where they need to have to courage to say no, to prioritize, and to focus their people. Without focus, change efforts get confusing, behavioral change stalls, and work efforts get diluted over too many projects. In the end, team members are forced to make decisions about what they believe is important, which may not be aligned with what the organization needs most.

In the book *The 4 Disciplines of Execution* by Chris McChesney and Sean Covey, the authors distinguish between the whirlwind and goals. The whirlwind is everything we do day to day to keep the business running. Too often, we try to change too much at one time within the whirlwind, to no avail. There's just too much going on.

The 4 Disciplines of Execution directs readers to narrow their focus to the area outside the whirlwind—your critical/wildly important goals—so that no one person, team, or leader has more than one or two wildly important goals at any time. Their research reveals that the law of diminishing returns is as real as the law of gravity:

- When individuals/teams have two to three goals beyond the whirlwind, they tend to achieve two to three goals.

- When individuals/teams have four to ten goals, they tend to achieve one to two goals.

- When individuals/teams have eleven to twenty goals, they tend to achieve zero goals.

In our work with leadership teams, we use a concept we call "sprint goals." Through a series of interactive discussions, sprint goals force a team to clarify and document their top three priorities for the upcoming quarter, creating clarity on what matters most for the organization.

Here's how you can create sprint goals in your organization:

- Have all team members write what they think their most important short-term priorities are for the team on separate sticky notes.
- Post them on a flip chart.
- Sort sticky notes into kindred groups.
- Facilitate discussion until the team narrows the list to their top three.
- Add target completion dates and discuss next action steps.

When we work with individual leaders to create individual behavior change, we take a similar approach:

- We gather verbal or online 360 feedback as a mechanism for leaders to see how others perceive them.
- We narrow the feedback into no more than two to three goals for a given ninety- to 180-day development period.
- We identify two to three specific behaviors that are most critical to driving these new behaviors.
- We relentlessly track perceived behavioral change over time through our Coachmetrix proprietary pulse-feedback process.

As an Evangelist of change, you have to create focus—for yourself and for others.

19 Operating at the Wrong Level

Stephanie sat down with Ben for his second of two quick quarterly check-ins. This was a more structured process than the informal group coaching sessions and the monthly one-on-ones she did with Ben, but it wasn't an annual performance review. Stephanie wasn't a fan of that and largely thought it was a waste of time. Instead, she created a culture of continuous dialogue: informal coaching through regular one-on-ones, quick quarterly reviews, and what she called a-ha moments. With those three building blocks of coaching, she was able to remove the annual performance review from BCO-Tek. It took a while before her leaders had the skills to coach on a regular basis and for everyone to adopt the mindset of coachability, but it was worth it. Stephanie believed that regular coaching was the underpinning of a performance-based culture and execution. With it, employees were always abreast of how they were performing and there were never any surprises.

"As you know," she explained to Ben, "when a leader is new to a role, about six months in, we conduct a simple 360 survey to gather feedback about your leadership."

"Got it," said Ben. "I know that you surveyed my direct reports, some of my peers, and a few others on the leadership team."

"The intent is to help you leverage your strengths and uncover potential blind spots by understanding how others perceive you." She handed over the 360 report, a few pages of survey data with strengths up front and opportunities for development in the second section. *"Take a few minutes to read through your strengths and then we'll discuss,"* Stephanie instructed.

Ben read through, making a few notes as he went. Then they talked about the key themes and patterns that were emerging. It wasn't surprising to Ben that he was perceived as an action-oriented, pioneering leader who got things done. People also appreciated that he challenged the status quo and had high expectations.

Then Stephanie had Ben look at section two. Again, he made notes, this time underlining various statements in the "opportunities for development" section. A few smirks and a squinted eyebrow or two later, he was ready to discuss.

"What are you learning?" asked Stephanie.

"Well," said Ben, his response coming a little slower than usual, "there's one primary theme that is obvious, about operating at the right level."

Among the comments that had struck a chord with him: "Ben may be the only person in the organization that can do something and it doesn't scale well. His perspective is that he has to do it. There's an opportunity to teach other people to think about the things that Ben thinks about."

Another comment caught his attention: "Allow people to make mistakes so that they can learn. Ben has been working hard on this, but he still has a tendency to come in and rescue others if he sees that something is destined for failure. Take a step back and let others learn and potentially take a different path."

"What are your reactions?" Stephanie probed.

"If I'm honest, these are accurate," said Ben. "For instance, I've worked hard on it, but I still have a tendency to dip back in and solve other people's problems."

"This is not unusual," Stephanie reassured him. *"At senior-leader levels, when you begin to take on responsibility outside of your technical expertise, there is a tendency to slip back into the roles in which you are comfortable. So, what do you think is the impact of that tendency?"*

"Like the first comment said, it's not scalable," Ben admitted. *"If I don't operate at a higher level, it forces my managers to operate at lower levels too."*

Stephanie pointed to the whiteboard. *"We're back on Mount Results,"* she said.

"At least are we near the summit?" Ben joked.

"Almost."

Empower your people and you will scale the business.

The second component of making the transition from *Task Manager* to *Evangelist* is empowering others. At the risk of sounding too consultant-y, we use this buzzword because it was the most cited word in our survey feedback. "Empowerment" was the common link between what executive leaders, senior leaders, and team members all suggested was important to successfully being a senior leader.

A challenge for senior leaders is that you are often overseeing work that isn't so familiar to you. For example, you might have started out as an HR generalist or recruiter, or compensation specialist, and now you are running the entire HR department with managers under you running each of those functional areas. Or maybe you are a sales leader who now owns all of Sales *and* Professional Services. A common tendency among senior leaders is to slide back into their comfort zone of technical knowledge and put more emphasis on areas where they used to be the "doer" of the work.

During a recent coaching engagement, we worked with a senior leader responsible for a software development and quality assurance team. The leader was struggling with providing growth and development opportunities for the quality engineer, as his expertise was in coding software. We coached the leader to consider the following:

Put the onus on the quality assurance engineer to find development opportunities based on the engineer's specific career path.

Use quarterly goals or OKRs (Objectives & Key Results) to track performance of both work output and development and learning.

Provide coaching in other critical areas that the leader is fully capable in, such as business knowledge, industry knowledge, coachability, and personal attributes that could derail a team member.

The bottom line is that to successfully empower people at the senior-leadership level, the Mindset Shift has to change from seeking stability to being comfortable working with ambiguity, and then applying the right level of hands-on or hands-off management to ensure results get delivered.

20 What's the Score?

Darryl thought it would be good to get out of the office and do something social with his and Ben's teams so they could let off steam. He and Ben picked up some last-minute tickets for the next afternoon's Colorado Rockies baseball game in downtown Denver. They announced it at their team meetings, and everyone was excited for the welcome break.

The next morning, just before 11 a.m., they car-pooled over to the Regional Transportation District, the RTD, to catch the 11:14 bus to Union Station. It was an easy thirty-seven-minute ride and spirits were high. The Rockies were having a moderately good season, and it was beautiful fall Colorado weather, with sunny skies and highs in the low seventies.

After a quick lunch at Union Station, they walked a few blocks to the game for the 1:10 p.m. start. It was a longer walk than expected, so they missed the first half-inning, but no one seemed in a hurry. They wandered across the Rooftop, an area in center right field that provided general admission tickets. Seating there was less traditional than stadium seating. It felt more like an outdoor roof-top bar with views of a baseball stadium. It was a perfect setting for a large team-building event, although less ideal for the baseball enthusiast who cared about every strike and ball count.

"Here's to Darryl," Ben said as he raised his plastic twenty-ounce can of Coors. "Thanks for the suggestion."

"Hear, hear," said Kevin.

"Yeah, thanks," said one of Darryl's team members. "I got my exercise getting all the way here too. What a schlep!"

Afternoon games on the Rooftop deck were usually crowded, especially on a nice day, and not everyone had a seat with a view of the field. They were about as far from home plate as one could be and still be in the stadium.

"What's the score?" asked Sandy, a product manager on Darryl's team.

Ben leaned a little left to see past the pole and some people who were obstructing his view. "I'm not sure who's winning," he said. "I can't see the scoreboard."

"Ha! Sounds like work," said Sandy with a friendly smile. "Just kidding."

Ben knew, though, that there was some truth in what Sandy said. Maybe people didn't know if they were winning or losing in the workplace.

That had to change.

Keep score using lagging and leading indicators.

In sports, the coach, team members, and fans always know the score. If they don't, they know just where to find it—on the jumbo screen at the stadium, or front and center on their television, or at the touch of their smartphone. Imagine how weird it would be not to know the score at a sporting event until late in the game.

In the workplace, it's different. Sometimes people understand the big picture and how they fit into it. Most of the time, they don't. When it comes to daily work on any given day or play, they're not sure if they're winning or losing.

Evangelists keep track of and communicate the score. They measure everything, using leading and lagging indicators, to understand the state of the business. They also keep track of "softer" measures, such as individual behavioral change of themselves and others on their team.

Here are two primary types of measurements to drive your score keeping:

Lagging Indicators: These are the results shown after an action or series of actions. It's the effect after the cause. Have you ever watched the weight-loss reality TV show *The Biggest Loser*? During each weekly weigh-in, contestants step on the scale to record their weight loss. They are effectively measuring their lagging indicator—the result of what they accomplished from the previous week of working out with their trainer and eating nutritionally. This is good information to have and is important to track. The only problem for those contestants is what is described in *The 4 Disciplines of Execution*: the lagging indicator doesn't provide predictability. It doesn't help people predict whether they are on track with enough time to adjust.

Leading Indicators: These give us information ahead of time so we can make adjustments along the way to ultimately have an impact on the lagging-indicator result. Leading indicators are predictive in nature. *The Biggest Loser* contestants measure two leading indicators associated with weight loss throughout their week: caloric intake and exercise.

You might argue that there are things that cannot be measured. How can you possibly measure the change in leadership behaviors? Or the level of engagement in employees? Or whether the team is being more collaborative?

In cases where there aren't "hard" numbers, Evangelists turn to qualitative measurement to track progress. For example, in our executive-team development programs, we create a team scorecard using Coachmetrix. Items on the scorecard might include how well the team is following its norms or aligned around key goals or engaging in constructive conflict. Then, on a monthly basis, team members pull out their mobile devices in the middle of a team meeting and provide pulse feedback based on the scorecard items. The team's metrics display immediately on the Coachmetrix Website. When projected for all to see, it can lead to meaningful discussion.

If you are working on making individual behavior changes for yourself, you can also measure by creating your own individual scorecard. *E-Myth* refers to these scorecards as KPIs (key personal indicators). Marshall Goldsmith calls them Daily Questions. Essentially, you are reflecting on the most important areas for your personal and professional development.

Here are the five questions I reflect on every day:

- Did I make progress toward my next book?
- Did I say NO today so I can focus on strategic work and thought leadership?
- Did I treat myself well? (nutrition, exercise, rest)
- Did I treat others well? (my wife, sons, team members, others)
- Did I address issues directly that "are not a big deal" today?

Evangelists are relentless about measurement. They know the score, and so do the people around them. The key here is to go from relying solely on gut feel to valuing the importance of measurement, discipline, and the structure it takes to make true change.

Chapter

21

Coach and Be Coached

Ben, Peter, and Darryl huddled for their next informal coaching session as Stephanie recapped what they'd covered so far.

"Making the shift from Task Manager to Evangelist requires you to (1) create focus, (2) empower your people, and (3) keep score," she said. "There are a few more components, but before we get there, tell me how you're doing with this shift so far. Darryl?"

Darryl didn't fumble as much as he usually did and instead responded with, "Struggling. As we've talked about, my tendency is to get into the weeds a little too much when it comes to execution. I don't always give things up because of my tendency to want to be accepted. Naturally, I don't want to overload my people." He paused a moment and then continued. "But the real problem is that I've been giving things up and trying to operate at the right level, and as I do more of that, I seem to be dropping the ball with things I used to manage more tightly."

"What do you mean?" asked Stephanie.

"Well, I have a team member who's a pretty high performer. He's putting good data analysis process in place to help scale the business, but in

many ways, he's overdoing it. He's building great systems for a Fortune 500 company, not a fast-growing $200-million company."

"Have you told him that?"

"We've talked about it a few times, very directly, which is unusual for me," said Darryl. "Frankly, he's not very open. He's tied to the solution he thinks is best, and when I offer suggestions, he gets defensive. But he's much more technically inclined than I am in this area. I'm not a data scientist."

"You're no rocket scientist either," said Peter.

"Oh, look who's getting comfortable in our little tribe!" Darryl jabbed back.

"This is a great springboard into the next element of making the shift from Task Manager to Evangelist," said Stephanie. "It's about coachability."

"Do you mean coaching others?" asked Darryl. "Or being coachable?"

"Both."

"Huh, interesting," said Darryl.

"How so?" asked Ben.

"Well, Stephanie always encourages us to coach our people, and she models it all the time for us," said Darryl. "It's just that, in the situation I described, I don't think this manager is coachable."

"Let me get this straight," said Ben. "You have a high-performing manager with more technical experience in this aspect of his role than you do, but he isn't open to feedback? Sounds like he needs coaching on his lack of coachability!"

"Exactly," said Stephanie. "Part of what an Evangelist does is to set the tone for the culture. Coaching people not just on performance but on attitude has to be part of that. Your team members can be technically smart, good producers, but if they aren't coachable, they can't be a top performer. Learning how and where to coach people is the lifeblood of a performance-based organization."

"A" players are always coachable.

The "coachability factor." Coachability encompasses a leader's ability both to see coaching others as "real work" and to being open to receiving coaching from others. Coachability is the foundation of performance-based cultures.

I've seen countless leaders and team members struggle with coachability—both in giving it and getting it. Perhaps it is human nature to want to avoid difficult conversations. But when we avoid giving team members feedback and coaching, we are doing a disservice to them, to the team itself, and to the organization as a whole. Senior leaders who fail to provide coaching also lose credibility and often fail to realize it.

At heart, people generally *want* coaching. They want to know what they are doing well and where they can improve. We've heard this from hundreds of people in our programs, and our survey results confirm it. And when coaching is provided in the spirit of helping people elevate their performance in the workplace, it is much more likely to be accepted in a positive manner.

For most senior leaders, the coaching effort is focused on the leaders they lead. It becomes less about coaching individual contributors. Inevitably, those leaders will struggle with the transition into leadership and will need help with key Mindset Shifts at that level. For example, as a senior leader, you will likely have to coach your managers to make the following changes:

Common Challenges as Manager	Possible Solutions / Goals for Your New Manager
Managing own time	Reallocating time to not only complete your work but also help align the work of others
Doing own work	Getting things done through others (for a larger percentage of the work you do)
Setting priorities for self	Establishing and communicating priorities for a team
Valuing technical skills / work	Seeing leading others as "real work"
Believing that doing the work is valuable work	Believing that making time for coaching others is a valuable part of being a leader
Solving problems for self and others	Enabling others to solve problems for themselves
Avoiding difficult conversations	Providing feedback on a daily basis

When Evangelists create focus, empower their people to do their jobs, and keep score, it becomes much easier to create an environment of accountability. The "difficult" conversations become less difficult and more about optimizing everyone's success.

If you have team members who aren't coachable, a yellow flag should alert you to focus your coaching efforts on helping those team members understand how this could ultimately derail their career.

22 Are We There Yet?

The monthly all-hands meeting had been an integral part of the BCO-Tek culture since early in the company's founding. Keeping everyone informed was the previous CEO's mission. Stephanie also thought it was important, and had kept up the practice, although she believed less in the impact of the all-hands meeting alone and encouraged ongoing dialogue every day by all her executive team members.

One of the changes Stephanie made was assigning a different member of her executive team to facilitate the monthly meeting. She felt it gave the other senior leaders ownership in the process and took some of the burden off her to make them interactive and creative each month. Now it was Peter's turn. A few minutes before the meeting, he entered through the main door of the large cafeteria area that took almost an entire bay in what used to be the warehouse. The concrete floors had been painted, and there were large tables made of reclaimed wood from an old barn. Peter was pulling a carry-on suitcase with a boom box bungeed to the top, blasting the Queen song "We Are the Champions." He was fired up to announce the Q3 results. After all, almost everyone in the organization had some part in making them happen.

He started off with a loud welcome and then announced the better-than-expected earnings. He ended with, "We are the champions of this market!" Then he introduced the second speaker on the agenda.

After the all-hands, Stephanie huddled with Ben, Darryl, and Peter for their usual debrief.

"That was quite the show today, Peter," said Ben. "Not my style, but people sure were fired up."

"Thanks," said Peter. "It was a great Q3, and I hope everyone takes take some time to celebrate." It was customary for the all-hands facilitator to lead the debrief, so he asked them what else had gone well.

The group brought up a few points on how they engaged team members, pulled from questions they had sent out prior to the meeting, including to some of the front-line leaders.

"What can we do better next time?" asked Peter.

"How about a round of karaoke," Darryl jabbed.

"Different music," said Ben. "Bon Jovi, 'Dead or Alive.'"

"All right, gentlemen," said Stephanie. "One suggestion I have is that we don't declare victory too early. In fact, don't declare it at all. It sends the wrong message. We have to keep people focused on our long-term mission."

"In other words, don't let up on the gas?" Peter asked.

"Exactly," said Stephanie. "It's easy to get complacent just because we're at the top of our game and market right now. But there will always be another competitor who is more agile, more innovative, and hungrier. We can't let our guard down. And we have to maintain a sense of urgency."

Just as they were wrapping up, Ben's mountain-rescue pager went off. Ben didn't often leave work to head out on rescue missions, but this was an exception.

Maintain a sense of urgency.

"In the Battle of Iraq, the United States and our allies have prevailed."

President George Bush made this statement on the USS Abraham Lincoln off the coast of San Diego. It was on May 1, 2003. We completed our withdrawal of military personnel from Iraq in December 2011, more than eight years later.

It's easy to let down our guard, especially on long-term change efforts that require months and even years of effort. In the words of John Kotter, the godfather of change leadership and author of many books on the subject, including Leading Change, don't declare victory too early.

The Evangelist realizes the need to maintain a sense of urgency months and years into a change initiative. It's usually easy to create a sense of urgency up front with enough painful information or an aspirational approach that helps move people to action. It's more difficult a task to maintain that sense of urgency after months or even years have passed after executing on a plan—a product line pivot, a merger or acquisition, or a culture change initiative.

Evangelists have to find ways to create small wins along the way, reminding people of why the effort is needed. They have to use recognition efforts when they see behaviors that are aligned with where the organization is going. They have to continue to communicate the need to change. They have to recognize that people don't move to change through facts and logic alone, but they will when leaders call upon an emotion. That emotion might be painful, such as anxiety, fear, or concern. Or it might be more aspirational by creating excitement, confidence, and opportunity. Evangelists then show and tell people the right things that will drive the emotion and ultimately move them to new ways of thinking or doing something differently.

To truly maintain a sense of urgency, Evangelists have to value the time it takes to do all these things.

Reflection Questions – Mindset Shift 4: From Task Manager to Evangelist

Reflect on the following questions to help you make this fourth Mindset Shift from *Task Manager* to *Evangelist*:

- Do people have clarity on the top priorities in the organization and in your functional area?
- Have you narrowed the top priorities to a select few?
- How empowered are people to make decisions and do their jobs?
- Do your people know if they are winning or losing by seeing visible leading and lagging indicators?
- Are you coachable?
- Do you coach others on a daily basis—especially the managers who report to you?
- Do you maintain a sense of urgency by appealing to emotions, leveraging recognition, and creating small wins?

Unite! The 4 Mindset Shifts for Senior Leaders

143

23 | The Final Mission

Ben was the first leader to arrive on scene. He'd picked up the truck and a few other rescuers from the team's headquarters just a few blocks from his office.

Eldorado Canyon, affectionately known as Eldo among local rock climbers, is a world-class rock-climbing destination on the outskirts of Boulder, just south of town. It attracts climbers from all around the globe. On this day, unfortunately—as on a handful of other days throughout the year—it was also the scene of a fallen climber.

Reports were that the climber had injured himself on a route called Ruper, a long, sustained rock climb on Eldo's largest climbing face, the Redgarden Wall. Ruper's moderate grade, with an intermediate rating of 5.8+, was often underestimated. It took an experienced climber to navigate the variable off-width cracks and run-out sections of climbing with little to no protection, not to mention having the courage to trust the wonky old pitons on the last pitch of the route.

As Ben and the others were pulling gear from the truck, John arrived. Being the senior leader on scene, he took Operations, a role designed to coordinate the overall mission. "Ben, can you organize a Hasty Team and start fixing the lower ramp?" asked John.

The lower ramp was a primary access point to Ruper. Its 200-foot, low-angle climbing was easy enough for Ben to solo. But he'd have to drag a rope and more gear to build an anchor so that other rescuers could use it to haul gear to the base of the route.

"I've got it," Ben responded.

"You're likely to be Site Lead once you get up there," John continued. "You ready?"

Ben didn't hesitate. He'd worked hard over the past few months to prepare for this moment.

"Ready," he said.

He pulled three other team members and signed out the equipment they needed. They began their hike to the base of the lower ramp. They crossed the bridge over the roaring South Boulder Creek below, followed a path along the creek, and then began ascending a series of switchbacks under the steep overhung climbing routes above called the Roof Routes. They arrived fifteen minutes later at the base of the lower ramp, after setting a blazing pace with heavy equipment on their backs.

"Hasty Team to Ops," said Ben, speaking slowly into his radio microphone, trying not to pant too heavily.

"Go ahead, Hasty Team," Operations responded. Ben could tell that it was John on the other end.

"We're at the base of the Lower Ramp, preparing to ascend and fix the rope." said Ben.

"Copy that."

Everyone knew their roles. Ben set the tone with a calm voice to make sure everyone understood the safety expectations. He inspected each person's harness, helmet, and other gear.

Ben was aware that when his adrenaline flowed, he tended to move faster. His breathing was more rapid and shallow. Being aware of these physiological reactions allowed him to take deeper breaths and slow things down so he could create a safer environment for himself and those around him. He was also aware of his environment and the potential for rock fall and other dangers. He also knew that instead of trying to look "smart" and play the hero, he would hand off fixing the rope to a more experienced climber, Dan. That also gave Ben a few additional precious minutes to think through next steps once they got to the top of the Lower Ramp.

It took Dan about five minutes to climb the Lower Ramp and another two minutes to build an anchor at the top. "Fixed line is ready," he called over the radio.

Ben clicked his radio mic twice, indicating that he understood the message while minimizing radio traffic. He pulled out his ascenders—climbing devices used to aid a climber up a fixed line—and attached them to the rope. Then he began climbing the Lower Ramp while the other team members followed.

When Ben reached the top, a flattish area that gave him some flexibility to move around, he could see the injured climber and about 150 feet above him, the climber's partner.

Ben made voice contact with the climbers. "Hello, we are from the mountain rescue team," he said. "Are you okay?"

A moment later, he received a response. "My partner took a pretty good fall on the second pitch." Pause. "I was able to lower him to the ledge that we're on, but it looks like he's pretty banged up."

Ben asked a few more questions to assess the situation, knowing that this was a "hurry-up."

"We need to get up there quickly," said Dan.

Ben refused to get sucked into the common trap of reacting too quickly and solving for only the presenting problem. He needed to think the mission through from start to end, because there were huge safety implications if he got any one step wrong.

He broke it down into three stages. "Dan, you're the lead on getting up to the climber, building the anchor, and getting the people and the equipment to the patient so you can lower the patient to our location here," Ben instructed. "Get on it and let me know if you need anything."

Remaining calm, Ben began his planning for Phase II. "Steve, you're in charge of organizing a litter team for the evac down the Lower Ramp. Jenny, find the right anchor and coordinate with Steve for the evac. You'll also take belay, so find a Rope Handler too."

Ben pulled back and radioed Operations. "Ops, Hasty Team Lead, over," he said.

"Go ahead," said John.

"I'll take Site Lead," said Ben, confirming what John predicted would eventually happen. "We're working on getting gear and people up to the patient. Looks like the patient is at the top of the first pitch, just above the Ruper Crack. Break." Break is a radio command that lets the receiver of the message digest the information that was just reported and also know that there's more coming.

"Go ahead," responded Operations.

"Reported injuries are a broken leg and other abrasions. Could be more severe. We'll have a full medical report once we get to the patient. Break."

"Go ahead," responded Operations once again.

"You'll need to assign a Site Lead at the base of the Lower Ramp to organize the evac down the switchbacks and across the river."

"Copy that," responded John.

Having thought through the entire plan, assigned roles, and considered the consequence of each stage of the evac, Ben was now ready to manage the overall execution of his three-phased plan. Remembering the practice mission just a few months back when he got overly caught up in the individual tasks, he resisted the temptation to jump in too deep. Instead, he reiterated the big picture to people who streamed onsite from the Lower Ramp, so they would have clarity on the vision for the mission. He checked in with each of his sub team leads—Dan, Steve, and Jenny—to make sure they were working on the most important priorities. He kept everyone apprised of the estimated time for the various stages of the evacuation to be completed.

"Ben," said Dan. "I'd suggest we send four people up with me to the climber. I'm going to need a 'third man' on the lower." Third man refers to a

rescuer who follows the descent of the patient and can offer additional support to deal with any rock outcroppings and unforeseen obstacles.

Ben considered Dan's perspective. That would mean putting one additional rescuer in harm's way. But he was also open to ideas—especially coming from Dan, a highly experienced and technically sound professional.

"Okay, take Adam with you," Ben responded, quietly proud of his own coachability in that moment. He knew that Stephanie would be proud too.

As the mission proceeded, Ben continued to use recognition and coaching to ensure that the environment was safe. After about forty-five minutes, the patient was packaged in the litter and lowered to Ben's location at the top of the Lower Ramp.

"Patient's down. Good work, Dan," Ben acknowledged over the radio. "Take your time getting back to the Lower Ramp and check your systems twice." Ben knew that Dan was feeling some relief. It was a relatively complex system he had to organize to get the climber into the litter and lowered down the 150-foot pitch. He didn't want Dan to get complacent just because the bulk of his role was completed. Ben had to continue to maintain a sense of urgency until every rescuer got out safely.

He considered the big picture again and called another experienced rescuer over. "Ted, here's the plan for the lower," said Ben as he laid out the details step by step. "What are we missing?"

Ben was still in his outcome orientation and thinking through not just the problem before him but the problem two or three steps down the line. Ted offered a few suggestions that Ben implemented immediately.

Another twenty-two minutes passed, and the patient was at the bottom of the Lower Ramp.

"Operations. This is Site," Ben said into the radio.

"Go ahead, Site," said John.

"The patient is at the base of the Lower Ramp. Scree Site is now in charge."

"Copy that," John replied again. "Double-check everything and take your time getting down."

Unite! The 4 Mindset Shifts for Senior Leaders

149

Unite! The 4 Mindset Shifts for Senior Leaders

Mindset Shift 1: From Smart to Aware

What is it? It's an enhanced state of awareness or *Interpersonal Agility*.

This Mindset Shift is about changing what you value and how you see your self-worth. Being smart is about having to prove your worth and demonstrate to others that you are the technical expert. "Smart" leaders tend to be less conscious of their impact on people, process, and the business. "Aware" leaders, on the other hand, ultimately have a deeper understanding of themselves and the impact they have on others. It's an understanding of the wake they leave behind when they lead others, so they can maximize their relationships. Aware leaders have clarity on the following:

- Why do others respond to them the way they do?

- Why do they respond to others the way they do?

- What in their environment is triggering the reaction they are currently experiencing?

Tool #1: The Self-Observer

- Step 1: Listen to your body.
- Step 2: Change your state.
- Step 3: Make a new choice.

Tool #2: Seek Feedback

- The verbal Likert scale
- The half-time adjustment
- 360 feedback
- Coachmetrix

Mindset Shift 2: From a Problem Orientation to an Outcome Orientation

What is it? This Mindset Shift in how people approach their work at hand.

Leaders with a problem orientation focus on solving one problem at a time. They see a problem and they fix it. They see another problem and fix that one too. It's a never-ending process of tension and relief as problems arise and the leader fixes them. The leader, usually without even knowing it, has a dysfunctional belief that leadership is about rescuing others instead of teaching, delegating, and coaching. These leaders are able to conceal their leadership weaknesses with their technical skills—usually very successfully!

Leaders with an outcome orientation broaden their perspective and take a more systems approach so they operate at the right level. It's an approach that requires leaders to (1) think beyond their own functional area, (2) consider a longer-term view, and (3) build people capacity.

Engage in cross-functional advocacy:

Considers multiple perspectives for solving issues:

1. Self: First, consider what your contribution is to the issue, challenge, or frustration at hand.
2. External: Second, conduct an external scan of what or who may be contributing to the issue, challenge, or frustration at hand.
3. Systems: Third, consider what system or lack of systems is contributing to the issue, challenge, or frustration at hand.

Drive strategic vision:

- Is a source of vision.
- Is a source of possibilities.
- Is a source for others to find greater meaning in their work.

Build people capacity:

- Selects the right people.
- Focuses on developing others.
- Thinks and plans for succession at all levels.

Mindset Shift 3: From Getting Compliance and Consensus to Winning Commitment

What is it? Overcoming style tendencies to win the hearts and minds of people so as to build commitment on your teams.

Aggressive leaders, like Ben with his laser-focused results orientation, tend to formulate their vision and immediately implement it. They are usually motivated by change, challenge, and controlling their environment and don't spend much time getting buy-in. Or, they recognize that they need buy-in and ask for input simply to garner support and not because they care about listening to what people have to say. As a result, people tend to be compliant with the pushy style instead of owning and being committed to the direction in which the organization will move.

On the passive side of the equation—think Darryl—the tendency is to be a people pleaser, where leaders are overly concerned about making everyone happy and gaining consensus from all the stakeholders. There's an avoidance tendency that comes with this style, as leaders tolerate behaviors that are unacceptable in the workplace.

Create structured and intentional communication:

* What is the key information that needs to get cascaded out to your organization?

* Who is the target audience?

* What do you want your audiences to do or think differently as a result of your communication?

* What vehicles / communication channels can we use?

* What is the frequency and cadence of that communication?

Communicate the Big Why:

* Discuss the alternatives that were considered.

* Tell people what you know and what you don't know—and why.

* Acknowledge how the decision will affect everyone.

Allow for dialogue:

* This is genuine and pure dialogue that gives people the freedom and opportunity to let you know the truth. This two-way conversation is where true interaction occurs as leaders engage people not just in formal settings, such as the all-hands meeting, but at every opportunity—from the chance encounter to the scheduled team meeting.

* The opportunity is to create a communication plan that employs multiple channels to engage people in the business and ultimately move them to a place where they know and feel they've been heard.

Mindset Shift 4: From Task Manager to Evangelist

What is it? It's about operating at the right level and truly letting go of task work.

There's a distinction between being a Task Manager and being an Evangelist for something. Managing tasks is important and critical work at every level within an organization, but as a guiding orientation, it's narrow, siloed, and mostly about getting things done. Being an Evangelist, on the other hand, is to be a supporter or a representative of a cause. While the Task Manager is focused on maintaining efficiency and the status quo, the Evangelist is focused on ensuring that the right things are being done in alignment with the vision and guiding direction of the organization.

Create focus

- Everything can't be a number-one priority.
- Create sprint goals.
- Focus your leadership development on two or three behaviors.

Empower your people to scale the business

- Be aware of a tendency to slip back to functional and technical comfort zones.
- Get comfortable with ambiguity.

Keep score

- Use leading indicators to provide predictive measures.
- Use lagging indicators to measure cause and effect.

Create an environment of coachability

- Be coachable and open to self-improvement.
- Coach others regularly.

Maintain a sense of urgency

- Continue to communicate the need to change. Remember that people don't change based on facts and logic alone, but mostly from emotion.

- Create small wins.

- Use recognition efforts to reward behavior that's in line with the overall vision and values.

About the Author

Sal Silvester is one of the top experts on leadership transformations across organizations and throughout careers. He is founder and president of **5.12 Solutions Consulting Group**, a firm that supports leaders and teams through grounded, real-world practices and techniques. Their cloud-based coaching platform, Coachmetrix, is the first of its kind to optimize and measure leadership development programs and coaching engagements.

Sal's unique perspective has been nurtured through his experience over the past twenty-five years as an Army Officer, an executive at Accenture, and the founder of 5.12 Solutions and Coachmetrix. He is a graduate of the US Army Ranger and Airborne schools and has led and managed teams in the desert of Kuwait, the mountains of Turkey, and in the offices of many clients.

He is an avid rock climber and mountain biker, has competed in six marathons, and is an Ironman Triathlon finisher. He's a member of Rocky Mountain Rescue, a nationally recognized search-and-rescue team based in Boulder, Colorado, where he lives with his wife and two sons.

Sal's blog, **www.512solutions.com/Blog**, focuses on helping ignite the potential of leaders and generating team member commitment.

You can find even more insights about executive coaching on his Coachmetrix blog at **www.coachmetrix.com**.

Other Happy About® Books

Stakeholder Centered Coaching

This book lays out the framework to help you generate better results from your coaching practice using a Stakeholder Centered Coaching approach.

Paperback $19.95
eBook: 14.95

The 24-Hour Turnaround (2nd Edition)

Empowers the small business leader or entrepreneur to steer a business to success, within the challenges of an uncertain economy.

Paperback $19.95
eBook: 14.95

CPSIA information can be obtained
at www.ICGtesting.com
Printed in the USA
FFOW03n2356281117
43802793-42713FF

9 781600 052699